# MOTHER BASHING

## Does She Deserve it?

## By

## Dr. Nancy E. Perry

Published by Sojourn Publishing, LLC

ISBN 978-1-62747-107-7 Paperback
ISBN 978-0-69234-421-7 Hardback
ISBN 978-1-62747-108-4 eBook

**This Book is dedicated to my mother**

**Estelle C. Reichard**

# Acknowledgements

With my deepest appreciation, I wish to thank all the people who helped me write this book. These include the many people in my pilot study who were willing to tell me about their pain related to relationships with their children and mothers. Many shared their problems and thoughts with me. My children, Karen, Scott, and Elaine gave me the inspiration for this book, as well as their encouragement and thoughts.

I am especially grateful to my husband, Richard D. Petre, PhD., who provided support throughout the whole process and was so helpful in the final editing of this book.

Others who helped edit the book and gave helpful comments, encouragement, and support were: Bernadette M. Rodriguez, who shared her perspectives as a single mother; Sandra Shaw, for her editing help; Ana Ekstrom, for her critical thinking skills; Amorette Deboer, who provided her perspective from someone in her 20's with no children; Cecilia Keough, who shared her many perspectives; Lee Starr, who communicated a keen appreciation for the book as it applied to her relationship with her own children; Barbara Cerino, for her support, understanding, and knowledge as a teacher, mother and daughter; and Eileen Sheil, Ph.D., who provided an analysis of the book from her perspective as a professor at the University of Wisconsin-Milwaukee.

# Forward

As a psychologist, a registered nurse, and mother of 3 children, I had originally believed that mothers caused practically everything related to their children. This included any psychological problems their children may have developed. Part of the reason I believed this was because of what I had been taught in graduate school. I soon began to learn how egotistical that idea was.

I believed that I, of course, would never be *"that kind of mother,"* the kind that causes their children to have problems. I thought that since I was so well educated and had not experienced a traumatic childhood, all would be well. I had pictured myself living in a "perfect house" with "perfect children," including a white picket fence around it all. I visualized my children as being well behaved, brilliant, and high achieving. They would love me forever, as I would love them. I had become part of the the psychological "Establishment" at that time and now admit with some embarrassment that I had actually believed that mothers caused almost all the problems that children experienced.

My awakening occurred one day, as I explain in my book, when I realized that one of my children held a grudge against me for something minor that had occurred more than thirty years earlier.

I suddenly awoke from my "all knowing" attitude and felt a growing compassion for other mothers who had been sharing their pain with me regarding their adult children, and children who had also been sharing their pain regarding their mothers.

I wanted to understand more about mother bashing and made the decision to discover what was true and untrue as well as discern the causes. I wondered if some mothers deserve to be blamed. The real world of today is so different from that of 20 years ago. These many changes have affected mother-child interactions.

I decided to write this book about the problems and solutions. I hoped to help others understand so they could have a platform to work from, to alleviate their pain.

I began by writing down my own thoughts and feelings and then asked other mothers to share their experiences with me regarding mother blame. I knew I must also consider all the past and recent research in order to make sense of this issue. I drew upon all my experiences as a mother and daughter and integrated these with my experiences and knowledge in the field of psychology. I decided to share some of my patient's experiences in order to communicate the points I felt were important.

First and foremost, I wanted this book to make a difference in people's lives. I hoped to communicate to the average person and avoid "psychobabble". As I wrote, I thought of you, my readers. I wanted you to know that I'm a mother too, and made a conscious decision to write this book from my heart as well as my head. One of my goals was to help children and parents understand each other better. Another was to provide some guidelines for healing. Yet another was to consider the impact on society as well as the world. As I wrote and researched and spoke with many mothers and children. It began to make sense.

# Table of Contents

# Introduction

This is a book about the causes of mother bashing and relationships between mothers and their adult children. Most mothers are women, but fathers as well as anyone may also fulfill the role of "mother". The book includes theoretical ideas, but is filled with examples from actual clinical cases that help clarify meanings. It is a book for everyone who has a mother or is a mother. It is for both men and women. Teenagers may find it a helpful tool to better understand themselves and their parents.

It is a very personal book. I have experienced mother blame in my own life as well as identified problems I had with my own mother. My own emotional pain launched me on the odyssey of writing this book. It drew me to unexpected places. I explored the possible causes of mother blame and, looked for ways to help improve relationships within families and help parents become more aware of factors in society that can be harmful to children. Many clinical cases are included in this book to illustrate some of the concepts presented here. The facts are true, but the identities and names of the people involved have been changed to protect their privacy.

As I wrote this book, I realized I needed to ask other people about their feelings regarding their own children and mothers. I spoke with 47 people about their experiences. It became a pilot study for the book. I learned that Mother Bashing or blaming mother has been part of our culture in the U.S. Society is guilty of unfairly blaming mothers for problems their children may have. Relationships between parents and children are often frayed. I became concerned about the effects of mother blame on mothers, their adult children, fathers, family relationships, and society.

The first part of this book defines mother bashing, explains what a good enough mother really is, explores some of the reasons society has blamed mothers and whether that blame was warranted, as well as addressing the normal, healthy aspects of mother blame as related to normal differentiation and individuation.

The second part of this book focuses on exploring the issues in our world today that can cause harm to developing children as well as factors that may cause conflict between mothers and children. Single parenting, child abuse, Social change, and the Technological Revolution can harm children. In my work as a psychologist, I have sadly witnessed many of these damages. As you read about these problems, you may find some of them shocking and difficult to assimilate, or you may disagree. So be it. These concerns come from my heart.

Children and parents may have different memories, causing great conflict. The way toward understanding this becomes clear in my chapter on memory.

The last part of my book recognizes the profound need for mothering at many levels, beginning with our own children and expanding this to the world. I designed it to help you assimilate what you learned about mother blame, as well as what you may have learned about yourself. Some mothers may decide they made some mistakes and feel some guilt; others may feel angry at either themselves or their children. Still others may realize they understand their mother or child better and feel uplifted or neutral. The last chapter gives concrete suggestions to help you deal with anger, learn to forgive if you choose, and begin to individuate to become your own person.

This book is not written to vindicate mothers or to blame them. Blame already exists. It is not a book about how to be a good parent, but it provides good parenting advice. It is a book that sheds a different light on mothering and parenting today and provides information about how to cope with discord in cross generational relationships. It invites mothers, fathers, and their children to evaluate themselves as they read.

Part of my odyssey involved developing a questionnaire to find out more information about what others are experiencing. You will find it at the end of this book. It can be taken on my website. I will use your feedback as data to scientifically explore the problems identified in this book and post the results on my website. I may use the information in one of my later books.

# Chapter 1

# BLAMING MOTHER

*A Fairy Tale*

*Once upon a time there was a princess who married a handsome prince. They were very, very happy and soon the princess discovered a baby was coming. There was great joy in the birth. Two more children followed. The prince and princess became a King and Queen and reigned over their kingdom, knowing someday their children would inherit it. The King was often gone as he needed to fight faraway battles to protect the kingdom. All was well. Then, one day, years later, the children grew up. As they got older, they became very happy with the Queen and King and decided to make the kingdom better than it had ever been. They were especially happy with the Queen because she had understood them since they were babies and had supported them in everything they had ever wanted to do and become. The Queen was very happy as she knew herself to be a good mother and she felt well loved. The King returned, triumphant from his battles. He was pleased with all the things the children and the Queen had done to improve the kingdom. The Queen was filled with joy. All her loved ones were together. The joy in her heart never went away. They all lived happily ever after. It has been said that situations like this occur in many kingdoms.*

T he above fairy tale depicts something that does not happen in middle class families today. This is due in part to present social and economic pressures placed upon middle class parents. I was stuck in that fairy tale!

In the last 50 years the roles of Mother and Wife have been transformed. Mothers, who traditionally have been blamed if something did not turn out well with their children, are often the victims of "Mother Bashing". Father Bashing occurs, but not to the same degree. For the purpose of this book, major focus will be placed on "Mother Bashing." In today's world, fathers are increasingly taking on the role of "Mother". However, most mothers continue to be women. Mothers have continued to be placed on the proverbial "Hot Seat" for anything that goes amiss with their children.

I was happily married, enjoyed and always wanted children. I had decided before I got married that I would be a "perfect mother". After all, I was a nurse at that time and looked upon myself as an "expert" in child rearing. Since my husband and I had always wanted children, we planned for them. I had studied all the latest books on the subject, taken developmental psychology courses, learned how to lead parenting classes, and decided which things I would do the same as my mother had done and which I wouldn't. I believed I knew all about the physical and emotional needs of children and at that time believed most problems with children could nearly always be traced back to the "mother". I had 3 children at that time. After my youngest child started school, I decided I could fulfill my dream to go back to school and to earn a Ph.D. in

Psychology. I later completed my degree and thought "all was well" with my family. I didn't realize I was living within a fairy tale. It wasn't until 20 years later that I realized all had not been well.

I remember the shock I felt when one of my adult children began to communicate negative things to me about what I had done when she was growing up. It began one day when she had been having difficulties in her own life. She came to me and announced that I had, "not been a good mother." I still remember the pain of that announcement. When I questioned how I had failed her, she stated, "You never carpooled me when I had to go to Girl Scouts and I had a winter jacket that had stuffing that had fallen down to the bottom and when I told you I was cold, you said I should wear a sweater under it". She believed her life had been ruined. What she said about the carpooling and sweater were true, but I felt confused about how such an insignificant event from the distant past could upset her to that degree. I felt misunderstood and believed she did also. I remembered that at that time I was in the middle of writing my doctoral dissertation and was not as sensitive to her feelings as she would have liked.

My daughter's complaints seemed somewhat trivial to me, but I realized she was experiencing a great deal of emotional pain about those events. I, at first, felt somewhat defensive, but wanted to understand what had happened between us and why. I discovered that many other mothers and adult children were experiencing similar emotional upheavals.

Her comments launched me on the odyssey of writing this book. They drew me to unexpected places to explore the causes of mother bashing. I considered the feelings of mothers who deserved blame for their adult children's problems, as well as the suffering experienced by children who had been emotionally or physically hurt by their parents. In the beginning, I realized I was somewhat biased as I had hoped to vindicate mothers. Soon after I began, I realized the magnitude of the issues and problems involved.

I decided that it was important to identify all the factors in today's world that can be potentially harmful to children as well as other causal factors in relationship problems between mothers and adult children. Although this book provides helpful information on parenting, its major focus is on the search for discovering the causes of mother bashing and understanding the pain in relationships between mothers and their adult children.

I had never consciously blamed my mother for any of my problems in life, but as I examined my life, I realized that I was also upset with my mother for some things she had done that had hurt me as a child and were still affecting me in my adult life. As I began to question other mothers and adult children, I realized both groups had experienced a lot of emotional pain in their relationships with each other.

Mothering today has changed. It not only includes mothering by a birth or adoptive mother, but may involve varying constellations of family organization. These constellations may be: single parenting by a man or woman, a married couple, parenting by relatives such as grandparents or aunts and uncles, combined parenting with parents as well as relatives and friends, lesbian and gay parenting. All of these constellations can work. The common thread in all groups who are successful in raising healthy normal children is the presence of a "mother" or "mothers" who are committed to raising children with love and commitment to permanent ties. Successful child rearing demands mothering

Mother bashing is defined as blaming mothers for something they said or did that had such a negative impact on their children that they believe it affected their lives in a significant negative way. I wondered, "Do mothers deserve it?"

## Blame

Blaming is known to be a response to something fearful or unpleasant. It is something we do in order to feel safe. For example, if a friend or family member gets cancer, it is normal to search for blame. We may think they did not take care of themselves and blame them, or perhaps we blame the doctor, or the food supply. That way we feel safer and more in control of not getting cancer ourselves. When things do not turn out well for us and we are unable to admit our mistakes and take responsibility for them, we might blame someone else for not helping us or hurting us in the past. Blame can be either healthy or unhealthy. Healthy blame is actually a stimulus to finding an actual cause for something using scientific methods, such as what actually causes cancer. Unhealthy blame is to blame something or someone to avoid taking responsibility for ourselves, or to make us feel better emotionally.

As I began to think about my mother, I considered what problems in my life were caused by her. I realized that there were two problems I believed my mother had caused.

My mother had grown up during the depression and was extremely fearful about not having enough money. She was obsessed with saving money all during her life and was thrifty to the extreme. She was also deeply concerned with her weight as well as mine. She monitored everything I ate and critically weighed me every week from the time I was a child to make sure I was not getting "fat". At that time I was skinny. I rebelled about the food and as a teenager paid for sweets from my baby sitting earnings and eventually got fat. Looking back at that situation and analyzing it, resulted in my awareness that my eating behavior was a rebellion against my mother's control. A later positive outcome was that my ability to rebel later gave me the courage to follow my passions in my life's work.

My mother's preoccupation with having enough money also sometimes affected me in a negative way, but ultimately also had a more positive outcome. My rebellion against the importance of money allowed me to focus on what I believe is one of the most important in life, which was to follow my heart and choose a career I loved. I wanted to help others as a nurse and later as a clinical psychologist. In order to pursue these careers I needed to minimize considerations as to whether or not I would earn a lot of money. This had a positive outcome for me as I learned if you do what you love, you will do it well and usually make adequate money.

I continued to blame my mother for my overeating, and lack of self-control with food, but was finally able to overcome using food to deal with any stress in my life, so I forgave her for that, believing that she only had my best interests in sight when she had been consistently obsessed with my weight. However, I found out I was not "home free" about the money issue one day after I was newly remarried.

I wanted to add some landscaping to our new home and my husband said kindly, "I don't think we can afford it." I felt my stomach knot up, I gritted my teeth, I could feel my blood pressure rising and I was not sure for a few minutes if we should have married. He was as astounded at my intense reaction as was I. I recovered after about 15 minutes of self-observation and when we tried to figure out what had triggered this, I realized I was still reacting to my mother's anxiety and my ingrained reaction to concern about money.

My weight problems were more difficult to solve. It took me many years to realize why I had become obese. My weight had continued to yo-yo for years until I realized I had been rebelling against my mother whom I loved.

Looking back at the positive and negative things my mother had done, I realized the positive outweighed the negative. I had always felt loved and had been encouraged to be the person I wanted to be. She taught me to take responsibility for my decisions early on. I realized that everyone has "mother baggage" as well as baggage from all early experiences. That is normal and necessary to learn and grow. Learning how to become aware of your baggage and how to let it go is a lifetime process for everyone. I knew my mother had been an imperfect good mother and had always believed she had done the best she could to parent me.

I began to wonder about motherhood in general and realized that no person, including myself, is perfect, whether a mother or not. All human beings are on their own paths. I started to question and become more aware of the negative opinions about mothers in the research, the media, and by some comedians who often used mothers as the butt of jokes.

The shock, hurt, sadness and anger I experienced after my daughter's accusations that had seemed so trivial were difficult to understand. I wondered if other mothers had similar experiences. I discovered that since I had planned to be a "perfect" mother, any complaint tapped into guilt about my lack of perfection. I searched my soul and remembered how much energy and love I had given to my children, knowing I had never abused them and had taken care of them in the best way I knew how. I had even been teaching parenting classes at the time of the carpooling incident. I briefly felt ashamed and believed I may have failed in achieving one of the things that was most important to me in life, raising happy self-fulfilled children. Then, as I let go of my guilt, I became even more determined to discover what was going on between mothers and adult children that was causing so much emotional pain for almost all the people I knew.

I decided to begin exploring all of the things that can cause children to have major problems in their lives and determine if mothers were to blame and if so, how? I wondered about the emotional pain both children and mothers experience with each other. Distress between children and mothers affects fathers as well.

I was knowledgeable about Child Abuse, as I had worked with child abuse and trauma victims for years. I wondered about what the difference was between being an imperfect mother and an abusive one. Part of me may have been still living within the fairy tale as my mindset had begun by thinking of motherhood in a traditional way, with a married couple living happily ever after.

I decided to do more informal research to better understand mother blame and discover if others had emotional pain related to their mothers or children. I considered it a pilot study and began to survey my clients; my friends, strangers, both men and women, as well as everyone I could find, to better understand mother blame. I asked them about their experiences as mothers and as children. I tried to determine who mothered their children and what their stresses were. I spoke with single mothers, gay and lesbian parents, traditional couples, working mothers, stay at home mothers, mothers who had a lot of money, mothers who didn't, and mothers going through a divorce. I asked all of them how they felt toward their children if they had any. I spoke with mothers as young as 18 and as old as 75. I asked everyone if they blamed their own mothers for any problems they had. I asked women who never wanted children, "Why?" I developed a questionnaire in the process to determine the experiences of both mothers and adult children, including adult children-who had never had children.

After I spoke to 47 men and women, I decided to continue pursuing the ways mothers could harm their children as well as societal influences that affected children negatively. I still wondered why children of good mothers blamed them in their adult life. I discovered that both mothers and adult children report the experience of a great deal of emotional pain in their relationships with each other.

## Good Enough Mothers

Although there are mothers and fathers who do abuse their children, most do not. Most mothers are what were identified by psychoanalyst Donald Winnicott as, "good enough mothers" or better. He believed the way to be a good mother was to be a "good enough mother." Winnicott realized that no human being is perfect. Perfection is impossible. Being a perfect mother is a myth. Mothers are real people. They pay attention to their babies and provide a consistent and safe environment. They offer both physical and emotional care as well as security. When they fail, they try again. They give their babies love, patience, effort and care. They are real human beings, under all the pressures and strains of life. They may have ambivalence about being a mother and may be both selfless and self-interested. They may be conflicted in their desire to turn toward their children or turn away from them, to be dedicated to them or resent them, to love them most of the time, or to hate them sometimes. These mothers are not boundless, but real. It takes an imperfect mother to raise a child well. Children need to learn that people are not perfect and they are not the center of the universe. They need to do things for themselves. They need to overcome their greed and need to learn and respect the needs and limitations of others, including their mother. They need to learn independence and know they are separate from their mother. In my early years, I actually believed I knew everything and could be a "perfect mother". I learned over the years that this is impossible and that I was and am far from "perfect". We all have our bad days when we are hurried, distracted, ill, have low blood sugar, etc.... Good enough mothers provide love, protection, consistency, respect, material safety and basic comfort. The most important of these is love. Good enough mothers on their bad days are still good enough. I decided that my mother was a good enough mother.

There are three basic components of good enough parenting. I have paraphrased M. Hoghughi's article from the *Archives of disease in Childhood* (1998) regarding the three basic tasks of good enough parenting as well as added a few of my own insights.

The first and most important is providing love, care, and commitment. Children need to feel that they are loved consistently and unconditionally. Physical contact, which includes cuddling and caressing as well as hearing their mother's vocalizations, is necessary in order to feel safe and loved. Attachment behavior is the natural consequence of this. An infant must become attached or connected to their mother more than strangers. If a child is severely emotionally deprived of this connection throughout early childhood, there is a risk of developing physical, developmental, and psychological problems. A lack of this bonding also causes emotional damage. A child who feels unloved and insecure begins to believe that he or she is unlovable. This may disturb character development. The following include some symptoms love deprived children may experience:

1. Lack of ability to give and receive affection
2. Self-destructive behavior
3. Cruelty to others or to pets
4. Phoniness
5. Stealing, hoarding, and gorging
6. Lack of long-term childhood friends
7. Extreme control problems
8. Speech pathology
9. Abnormalities in eye contact
10. Learning disorders
11. Lying

Lack of love can cause problems with relationships throughout life.

The second component is providing limits with the use of consistent setting of boundaries. Limits are concerned with setting and enforcing boundaries to help the child in his/her dealings with the outside world. We discipline them because we love them. Failing to discipline is failing to love. We discipline children to prepare them for life. Boundaries must be set to show what behavior is unacceptable, with due allowances made for developmental stages. Enforcement involves clear actions of either reward or disciplinary sanctions to ensure compliance within these boundaries.

"Good enough" limits require the setting of reasonable boundaries which are enforced in a consistent yet loving way that the child eventually accepts the reality of the boundaries and incorporates them in his or her actions. Ideally the child learns to live within generally acceptable boundaries for behavior, that is, becomes socialized. If the boundaries are inherently unreasonable or limits are applied inconsistently or too punitively, this will be damaging to the child's development. Children may also need to be protected from dangerous situations by setting boundaries. Many habitual delinquents have been the subject of an indulgent lack of discipline interspersed with unpredictable and sudden outbursts of harsh discipline.

The third component is facilitating the child's development. This involves fostering the child's development to enable the child to fulfill his or her full potential. It encompasses every area of functioning, from the physical and intellectual to the moral, aesthetic, and spiritual. Every child has a fundamental need for a secure base from which to explore the environment. "Good enough" care involves providing rich and varied stimulation in early childhood followed by involvement and support for the child throughout later years until adulthood is reached. Lack of this kind of enrichment prevents the child from reaching his or her full potential.

Mothers and adult children who are reading this may be evaluating themselves as well as their mothers as they decide if their needs were met as well as if they met their children's needs in a "good enough" way. Mothers in the changing world of today are called upon to not only be aware of the dangers their children may experience, but to deal with the societal stresses placed upon them as mothers.

## Blame by Society

As I continued my search to understand why so much mother blame was occurring, I realized that not only do mothers blame themselves, but society is responsible for blaming them also.

I remembered from my training as a psychologist the teachings of Sigmund Freud, the founder of Psychoanalysis. He and others believed that most of the problems people experience in their lives can be attributed to poor mothering. Over the years mothers were blamed for autism, sociopathic behavior, and criminality. Children's emotional problems were blamed on "poor parenting". Most of the blame was targeted at mothers. Freud's psychoanalytic theories provided a basis for this. Freud thought women were less capable than men in the area of morality and that most women over 30 were already beginning to show signs of being exhausted by life and therefore a child needs his father to protect him or her from future problems.

American psychiatry in the mid-twentieth century was based to a large extent on environmental or nurture beliefs as a cause for all types of mental illness. Psychiatrists believed that early childhood experiences were the cause of schizophrenia. Focus was mainly placed upon the mother. In the American Journal of Psychotherapy John Neill, M.D's article in *the American Journal of Psychotherapy* (1990) chronicles the rise and fall of the concept of the "Schizophrenogenic Mother". This phrase was coined by Frieda Fromm-Reichmann, in 1948. She blamed mothers for schizophrenia. Psychoanalytic theories had a definite antifeminist bias. Freud's writings display a pervasive ambivalence that is the direct product of his ambivalence about and anxiety concerning women. Even though many of his theories about parenting, women, mothers, male superiority, and sexuality have been disproved they still have a negative influence on attitudes toward mothers today.

## Nature versus Nurture

When I thought about children who might blame their mothers for their problems when they grew up, I considered adults who have problems such as criminality, emotional problems, relationship problems, autism, and learning problems.

Another reason society has had negative reactions to mothers is related to the long debate about whether children inherited their social tendencies or if what happened to them after birth caused them to be the way they were. There has been a real trend for the last 50 years to believe that children come into the world as "blank slates" and good parenting can overcome inherited characteristics.

## Individual Differences in Infancy

Proponents of the blank slate theory have ignored unmistakable evidence that children are individuals from birth. Every mother who has more than one child has experienced this truth. The blank slate theory proposes that all children are the same at birth and whatever they become is a result of their experiences.

Of course an environment with good parenting does help children develop to their optimum potential. However, there is research to indicate that heredity is also important. Extensive research with newborn infants has discovered differences in temperament, intelligence, ability to focus their attention, visual attention, cognition and spatial cognition. These differences in infants can have an effect upon a mother's responses to her infant. An example would be: an infant who rarely cried might not get as much attention from a busy mother as an infant who was more demanding. Mothers may tend to feel more connected to a child with similar qualities to herself or himself, and could subconsciously behave differently as a result.

Twin studies indicate that some identical twins that were raised apart in separate homes and had never met each other were alike in looks, intelligence, food preferences, occupational interests, and life choices in adulthood. Some of them had married at almost the same age and even had spouses of the same name. Some studies of criminality have also demonstrated a hereditary component.

Mothers are also not "blank slate" individuals. Each has her own interests, abilities, limitations, baggage, temperament, emotional intelligence and energy level. Acceptance of individual differences in both children and mothers impacts our understanding of how relationships between mothers and adult children may become stressed.

I sometimes think about Eleanor. Eleanor was a mother who was totally dedicated to her family. She was married to a physician who worked many long hours and was unable to spend much time with her or their children. Eleanor spent most of her time providing care for her children and keeping the family home in good order. She called me one afternoon and asked for an appointment. She said, "I only need one or two appointments, but I must talk to someone soon!" Her voice sounded tearful and desperate. I saw her two days later.

As soon as Eleanor sat down she blurted out, "I am at my wits end. I have a little girl and I don't know what to do with her!" I wondered what her problem could be. As I questioned her further, Eleanor began to cry and told me her daughter was "too good". As we talked, Eleanor told me she had 3 children. The first two were boys and the third was her daughter Tiffany.

Eleanor described her boys as very "active". Sam, the oldest was now 7 and in school. She sounded proud when she told me he was in the second grade and already reading at a fifth grade level. Sam, as an infant had been "difficult" as he was actively exploring the world and demanded a lot of attention. She mentioned that he loved her cooking. Edward, her second son was 5 and in kindergarten. Eleanor beamed as she described how he enjoyed kindergarten and could already read. She said he was interested in "everything", especially how mechanical toys worked. Eleanor described him as active also, but more "cuddly". He loved sitting on her lap when he was tired or not feeling well. When he was an infant, she said he had cried a lot. Eleanor felt needed by both the boys. Her descriptions sounded like good connections had been made between Eleanor and her boys.

Eleanor then began to describe Tiffany. She shed tears when she said she had always wanted a little girl and was thrilled when Tiffany was born. It seems her first major problem was that Tiffany did not cry as an infant. This seemed hard to believe. Eleanor said she would always remember Tiffany's first night home from the hospital. She put tiffany in her crib and went to bed herself, expecting to be aroused for a feeding in a few hours. Eleanor said she awoke 8 hours later and immediately realized Tiffany had not cried, or else she had not heard her. She raced to Tiffany's crib and found Tiffany "just lying there, looking at the ceiling". Eleanor decided to breast feed immediately and it seemed to her that although Tiffany nursed, she did not seem particularly hungry. Eleanor then waited until 5 hours later. Tiffany was again just comfortably looking at the ceiling. Eleanor again fed her and cared for her. This pattern continued for a week and Tiffany had not cried once. Eleanor called the pediatrician and made an early appointment to see if anything was wrong with Tiffany because she never cried. The pediatrician could find nothing wrong and gave Tiffany an immunization. Tiffany cried for the first time. The doctor said this meant she was "just fine". As time progressed, Tiffany never initiated cuddling or feeding, leaving Eleanor to initiate them. As time progressed, Tiffany passed all the developmental milestones of sitting, walking, and talking. However, she never initiated explorations, but seemed to enjoy outings and cuddling. She had become a normal, somewhat shy little girl of age 2 when Eleanor spoke with me. Eleanor stated her problem as, "I love Tiffany, but feel like she doesn't fit into our family. She is like no one else in either my husband's family or mine. We are all interested in everything and go getters and outgoing. I don't know how to connect with her. I am not sure she loves me or needs me. I want to be a good mother to her and somehow I feel guilty."

Tiffany's temperament was extremely laid back and the rest of the family had temperaments more sensitive to sensory and motor stimulation. Essentially her personality was different from infancy to those around her. These differences initially presented problems for Eleanor, who admitted she felt "rejected" as a mother by Tiffany, who it seemed did not need her for food or comfort.

Eleanor did not understand that different infants have different temperaments, abilities, interests, and activity levels. A few sessions of therapy helped relieve her guilt and facilitated her acceptance of the differences between them. Eleanor eventually found ways to connect with Tiffany.

This case is important because it highlights the need for understanding that differences between mothers and their children can be extreme. It is normal to love all your children, but also normal to "connect" differently with all of them. Children are all different and mothers are also different. As children mature the interaction pattern with each child becomes unique.

These differences may cause problems within families that can create mother blame. Parents may be accused of favoritism. It is unavoidable to enjoy your connection with a child who relates to the world in the same way you do. It is normal to connect with a child when you feel that you are on the same "wave length". It does not mean you do not love all your children the same. Awareness of this dynamic may help you to be more sensitive to all members of your family and possibly avoid some possible conflict.

After considering the effects of individual differences between mothers and children, I turned my attention to a case involving criminality.

## Criminality and Heredity

I recalled the case of Susie. Susie was referred to me by the court. I called it "The Devil Was There" case, one of the most dramatic in my career. I was asked by the court to evaluate a six year old girl to determine if she had been abused by her mother's boyfriend, Boris. Cindy was Susie's mother. The judge asked me to evaluate Boris and Cindy as well. Boris had been on parole for $2^{nd}$ degree murder, and a complaint was made to the police by Susie's paternal grandmother who had found genital injuries on Susie's body while bathing her. Boris had been on parole and, after the complaint, was arrested and placed in jail. My work with Susie, in conjunction with reports of physical damage in her genital area by a physician, convinced me that Boris had indeed physically and emotionally abused her. She described in detail how she was sexually abused and said, "The Devil was there! Boris told me so!" Susie sobbed as she described how "it hurt" and volunteered the information that "There were candles all around". She said her mom was there too, "watching". After spending many hours with Susie, I went to the jail to evaluate Boris. The evaluation had to be done under armed guard. I had never before and never since, in my 30 some years of practice, found anyone with such a psychopathic personality. As I entered the room and looked at Boris, I felt a dark energy. I could feel the hairs standing up on the back of my neck. I interviewed him and gave him various psychological tests. His answers showed him to be a psychopath with no conscience and the capability of pure evil. He was also very intelligent, in the gifted range. The last thing he said to me was, "Dr. Perry, I'm not staying in here you know".

I had an appointment with Cindy for two days after my evaluation with Boris. I got word several hours before my scheduled appointment with Cindy that Boris had escaped from jail with Cindy's help. The police traced them to where they were hiding and, as they were surrounded by police officers, Boris grabbed Cindy by the hair, shot her in the head and then shot himself.

I was shocked and saddened. I wondered how this man had become who he was. Was it his early childhood? Was it his mother or father? What I discovered was very interesting. He had been given up for adoption at birth and was raised in a loving home. He had enjoyed every advantage growing up culminating in an excellent college education. Boris had earned a graduate degree. When looking further into his past, I discovered that his natural father, whom he never knew, was in a high security prison in another state and had been diagnosed as a psychopath. Both father and son were similar to Hannibal Lector in the well-known movie, "Silence of the Lambs".

In this case, heredity seemed to be clearly the cause of his criminality. Boris had good parenting. That is not to say that all criminality is the result of heredity, but a major part has a heredity component. There is research to indicate that parents who do not provide consistent loving discipline can produce delinquency. Good enough mothers do provide consistent loving discipline and can take themselves off the hot seat for lack of discipline as a cause for criminality in their children. In this case however, Susie's mother, Cindy, was not good enough. She was present when the abuse happened, did not protect Susie, had maintained her relationship with Boris, and had helped him escape. I never had the opportunity to get to know Cindy and I wondered how she could have sacrificed her child for Boris. All I was able to discover was that she had been married very young to Susie's father, later divorced, and had worked as a waitress.

After this case, I began to study criminal behavior in general. Many of the cases seemed to be the result of inheritance rather than parenting. Almost all of the cases I explored were not related to good enough mothering. I have worked with many people who have experienced abusive parenting and although negatively affected by it, turn out to be basically good people and not criminals.

## Blame by Literature

I wondered when society began to blame mothers for many kinds of problems. I traced some possible beginnings of negative influence related to societal blame to the book by Philip Wylie, "The Generation of Vipers", which was first published in 1942. Wylie coined the phrase "momism". This book may have been one of the initial stimuli for mother bashing. (Keep in mind that the book came out in 1942) At that time women had only just begun to work outside the home. Wylie believed that women were the cause of all social problems and that all they were interested in was money. He thought they used motherhood as an excuse to do "nothing". In his mind women were of low intelligence, uneducated, and useless. Hold on to your hats as you read some assorted quotes from his book!

"....The devil whispered. The pretty girl then blindfolded her man so he would not see that she was turning from a butterfly into a caterpillar. She told him too, that although caterpillars ate every damned leaf in sight, they were moms, hence sacred. Finally having him sightless and whirling, she snitched his checkbook. Man was a party to the deception because he wanted to be fooled about Cinderella. ....Mom's first gracious presence at the ballot box was roughly concomitant with the start toward a new all-time low in political scurvyness, hoodlumism, gangsterism, labor strife, monopolistic thuggery, moral degeneration, civic corruption, smuggling, bribery, theft, murder, homosexuality, drunkenness, financial depression, chaos and war. ....Knowing nothing about medicine, art, science, religion, law, sanitation, civics, hygiene, psychology, morals, history, geography, poetry, literature or any other topic except the all-consuming one of momism, she seldom has any especial interest in what, exactly, she is doing as a member of any of these endless organizations, so long as it is something."

This controversial book and other writings like it had a negative effect upon how the public viewed mothers. It is another causal factor to consider as to why mother blame has become so popular.

## Specific Childhood Problems Attributed to Mothers

I considered other specific problems that children may have, that have been attributed to mothers by society. One of them is autism. Mothers had been "blamed" by clinicians for this condition for years. Specific mothers had generally not been confronted directly, but we clinicians "knew" what really caused it. This was a result of the acceptance of Freud's theories. Now we know this is not true. There has been a rapid growth of cases of Autism and they are now thought to be caused by some physical agent such as food, drugs, or other environmental substance. Heredity, older fathers and older mothers have also been implicated. Mother is finally off the hook for causing autism.

I remembered my case, "The abandoned wife". Ginny was a young 24 year old women whose husband had suddenly left her. Their son Jon, age 2 had recently been diagnosed with Autism. Jon was unable to look anyone in the eye, spun around and around incessantly, and had no sign of speech development. (Both Ginny and her husband Joe had been devastated by Jon's diagnosis.) Jon was their first born child. Ginny and Joe had gone together to doctors and therapists to find out how to help Jon. They wondered what could have caused Jon's problem. A therapist told them it was probably something Ginny had inadvertently done during early parenting. Ginny thought it might be hereditary as one of Joe's distant cousin's had a son with autism. They began to blame each other. Their home quickly became a battleground. Joe packed his bags and left, telling Ginny that it was all her fault. Ginny became very depressed and anxious. One night she took an overdose of sleeping pills and was saved by her next door neighbor who came over in the morning. When no one answered the door, she got the spare key and found both Ginny unconscious and Jon in his crib. I counseled with Ginny for about 6 months to help her accept the loss of her husband, the guilt of thinking she may have caused Jon's autism, the loss of her dreams for Jon, and to help her find ways to handle being a single parent of an autistic child. Joe never returned and did not want to see his son. He did pay child support, but as far as I know to this day, He still blames Ginny for all their pain. This is another example of Mother Bashing, in this case by both society and Joe.

Mothers have been the butt of jokes in the U.S. for a long time. It seems that everyone has mother issues. Some questions mothers report asking themselves when accused of being a bad parent are: Is this fair or unfair? Why aren't they blaming their father too? How have I failed? Is it my partner's fault?

In cases when a child exhibits seriously negative behaviors such as breaking the law, serious irresponsibility, dishonesty, hurting others, serious emotional problems, or poor impulse control, mothers and fathers may find themselves asking: Did this really happen? Did I do a bad job of parenting? Did I cause it? Is it my fault? What did I do wrong? Could I have prevented it? Am I a bad person? What can be done now? Do I have the right to complain? What is the next step? Remember, in most cases, it was not your fault! Most of us are good enough mothers! Good enough mothers do not cause these problems. Children's bad behavior may be caused by hereditary influences, influences of TV or the internet, child abuse, physical problems, peer pressure, unavoidable changes within their families such as death of a parent, divorce, illness, and Social Change.

During my pilot study, I informally spoke over the last few years with many people as to whether their mother has said or done anything that they believe has damaged them in their life? Or whether they have been given feedback by one or more of their children that they had done or said something to their child before the age of 18 that the child believes has caused damage in their life. I asked about the effects of blame on their relationships with each other. Most people answered yes to both questions unless the parent had died before the child was totally independent. People from certain ethnic groups seemed less apt to blame their mothers or have had their children blame them for their problems. These ethnic groups were Latin, Italian, and Jewish. The people I spoke with all lived in the United States. More research needs to be done to compare what is going on in the U.S. to that in other countries and within different ethnic groups as well as to validate my pilot study results.

## Major Factors Placing Blame upon Mothers

I continued to identify all the factors that have placed blame upon mothers. It became evident that they fell into 3 categories.

The first category included false societal beliefs such as belief in environment as the primary factor in child growth and development, the belief that "normal" imperfect responses by a good enough mother can be the causal agent to ruin a normal child's life, belief in the theories of Sigmund Freud and psychoanalytic theory as well as some of the media such as the book, Generation of Vipers which expressed the belief that single mothers cannot be good enough and are somehow irresponsible and naive.

The second category included factors outside of parental control that actually harm children and may have a major effect on their life and development. These are the various forms of child abuse, single parenting, influences from the development of technology, and social change. Good enough mothers do not abuse their children and need to understand the differences between "hard core abuse" and an occasional inevitable negative interaction with their child. It is becoming more difficult to be a good enough mother with all the stresses upon mothers created by social and technological change.

The third category, and perhaps the most difficult to remedy, is self-blame. Good enough mothers may feel guilty if things do not turn out well with their children or if their children are in trouble. They may also feel guilty because they are not "perfect". This type of guilt may be perceived by the child and used as a tool to manipulate their mother. When this occurs, Parents may be controlled by the child who knows how to make his or her mother feel guilty and therefore more vulnerable to manipulation.

I worked with a family that had been devastated by this dynamic. Michael and Carla had been married for 30 years. They had 1 son, Harold. The family came to counseling because the couple was thinking of getting a divorce and had been arguing about what to do with Harold, age 29. He was their only child and still lived at home with them.

Harold had a college education, but had been unable to keep a job. He claimed that everything "bored" him. He insisted on staying home and played on his computer most of every day. Carla cooked his favorite foods, cleaned his room, and did his laundry. Michael grudgingly provided him with spending money. At the time they came for counseling, Harold was complaining of being "too nervous" to find another job. He blamed his parents for his nervousness and was very upset because Michael had been losing patience with him. Michael believed that Carla had treated Harold like a baby all his life, and now it was time for him to "grow up". When Michael wanted to go on a trip with Carla, Harold would start having panic attacks and Carla believed if she was a good mother, she should not leave him.

During therapy sessions it became clear that Carla had always tried to be the perfect mother. Harold had learned how to manipulate her to get whatever he wanted. Carla admitted to being "filled with guilt" every time Harold was unhappy. She had sacrificed her life to "keeping Harold happy". Harold had also suffered the loss of a normal life up to that time. He had most of his needs met by manipulating his mother. This had almost destroyed his parent's marriage.

Therapy took 3 years. Everyone was referred for individual therapy. I proceeded with couple's therapy and occasional family therapy. All the therapists worked as a team. Carla and Michael did not divorce and slowly built a comfortable alliance and a life of their own. Michael was not allowed to live with them and was forced to support himself. He worked out his nervousness with his therapist and finally began to take responsibility for himself. Carla had to learn to let go of her guilt, accept herself as a good enough mother and stop blaming herself.

Another way mothers experience blame is through criticisms made by adult children of good enough mothers focused on their mother's imperfections. This is sometimes based on inaccurate memories or influenced by problems the adult child is having in his or her current life. It could also be based on misunderstandings between mother and child that occurred many years ago.

Mothers must not only be taken off the "Hot Seat" for all the problems children experience, but stop blaming themselves for everything negative that happens to their children. This can occur when mothers let go of their guilt and realize they cannot control all aspects of a child's life, even though they may try to protect them from all possible danger.

Even though mother blame is unfair to the average mother, many mothers continue to blame themselves for their children's errors. If they know they have loved their children, provided for them physically and emotionally as humanly possible, protected them from known dangers, never knowingly hurt them in any way and, although not perfect, had always been there for them, they can let go of their guilt.

Some mothers may discover that they were to blame for some of their children's problems. If that is the case, it is important to face that reality and decide how to deal with your knowledge. It may be helpful to find a counselor to support you in this process. Part of the process is forgiving yourself, making amends, and moving on.

Sometimes mother blame is a way for a child to differentiate from his or her mother in order to gain independence and feel free to explore new horizons to discover who they really are.

# Chapter 2

# DIFFERENTIATION AND INDIVIDUATION

*On Children*

*Your children are not your children*
*They are the sons and daughters of life's longing for itself*
*They come through you but not from you,*
*And though they are with you yet they belong not to you.*
*You may give them your love but not your thoughts*
*For they have their own thoughts.*
*You may house their bodies but not their souls,*
*For their souls dwell in the house of tomorrow,*
*Which you cannot visit, not even in your dreams.*
*You may strive to be like them*
*But seek not to make them like you.*
*For life goes not backward nor tarries with yesterday.*
*You are the bows from which your children*
*As living arrows are sent forth.*
*The archer sees the mark upon the path of the infinite,*
*And he bends you with his might*
*That his arrows may go swift and far.*
*Let your bending in the archer's hand be for gladness;*
*For even as He loves the arrow that flies,*
*So he loves also the bow that is stable.*
*(On Children by Kahilil Gibran)*

T he above poem, published in 1923 in the book The
Prophet, depicts so well a mother's and father's task

31

as well as the awareness that the future is unknown that we can really not be part of it in the same way as our children. If we do our job well, we will not only let our children differentiate from us and no longer be part of us, but spur them on to become who they are.

I had been shopping early one day and saw a big sale on men's shirts. My new husband of 1 year and I were going to a party on the following weekend where everyone was supposed to wear yellow. I spied a yellow shirt on the sale rack in his size and thought how happy he would be if I bought it. It would be a little surprise! I arrived home with the package and when he met me at the door, handed it to him and said, "Surprise! Look what I bought for you on sale! You can wear it this weekend!" He first turned pale, then, his face got red. He was furious and said something like, "How could you do this to me? I told you I don't like clothing as gifts. I don't want anyone to tell me what to wear!" I was shocked and first became angry, then tearful. After all, I was a "psychologist" and was supposed to know how to handle everything "perfectly". I didn't know how to respond to him, so I told him I would go to my home office to cool off and maybe we could talk about it later. After several hours, I emerged and we met in the living room. He looked sad and distraught. He said, "I'm sorry. You didn't deserve that. I've been thinking about why I did that. It's my mother. She always told me what to wear and gave me gifts of clothes that I hated. When I grew up, I would never let anyone buy me clothes or tell me what to wear". We made up of course and better understood each other as a result.

He was blaming his mother. Perhaps he was still working on differentiation.

At that time I had been preparing a talk about child development and how experiences affect intimate relationships with others in their adult lives. The conflict with my husband helped me remember how I had experienced differentiation from my own mother. My mother always believed she would die young and had been obsessed with her health. Even though she thought she would die at an early age, she worked outside our home as an accountant for 8 hours each day. I loved her dearly and when she told me one day when I was about 5 years old that she wanted me to learn how to do everything on my own because she would probably die soon, I was devastated and became very anxious. I believed her. Now I know that is when I began to become my own person and truly separate from her. In retrospect, I realize how traumatic this was, but it also set the stage for me to later be free and have the choice of individuating myself to a greater degree as I progressed through life. She lived a full life to the age of 97.

We all have difficulty differentiating or separating from our mothers. Some mothers also have difficulty differentiating from their children. We must accomplish this in order to begin to know who we are and have glimmers of who we can be. After we separate or differentiate, knowing we are different from our parents, we can begin to individuate and discover what is hidden in our psyches. Carl Jung wrote about individuation and described his life long process of finding out who he was. Some people choose to continue this process throughout their lifetimes. I chose to continue the process and am still "finding out" more about who I really am. Others are uncomfortable with that high a degree of separateness as they get older. It is an individual choice.

## Definition of Differentiation and Individuation

Margaret Mahler, a Hungarian born psychiatrist is best known for her Separation-individuation theory of child development. She described infants perceiving themselves as one with their mothers and progressing slowly through sub phases to discover their own identity, will, and individuality.

As I thought about my own process of individuation, I remembered back to when I graduated from college at the age of 21. I had studied nursing and earned a B.S. degree. I thought I knew myself and everything I needed to know for the rest of my life. I loved giving advice to everyone about everything and was quite a "know it all". I must have been unbearable. It took a lot of hard knocks to become humbled and realize I had barely "just begun". I slowly learned that I knew almost nothing. I had just begun to individuate.

I've realized that differentiation from our parents is just the first step that enables us to begin to individuate or become who we really are. Individuation is an exploration into our own psyches. It is the cultivation of mindfulness or awareness of what we are feeling and how we are behaving and why. It can open us to new awareness' s and ideas. It may cause us to feel different from those around us. It can become an ongoing lifetime process. I could understand what Carl Jung meant when he spoke of his loneliness and feelings of separateness from those around him as he individuated. Human evolution cannot truly evolve unless some individuals are courageous enough to deal with this loneliness as well as risk disfavor with the "establishment".

I remember feeling anxious when I decided to go to graduate school and leave the normal role at that time of wife and mother. Part of my continued search inside myself was the result of my desire to become a good therapist. I discovered the most amazing things that I am only now beginning to share. Many things I was afraid to share for fear of personal rejection or disfavor. Individuation may be end point some of us may reach in our lifetime. Some people call it "enlightenment". As we look at our own beginnings, we can consider where evolution of our children's development may take them.

During the time an infant is growing inside his or her mother, there is also a special emotional bond growing between the two. To varying degrees, mothers report feeling as though their infant is actually part of them physically and emotionally. This is different from the bond between fathers and infant. Many fathers report feeling a connection with their growing infant before birth and a more complete love after their child is born. This is different from what a mother experiences. The bond between mother and child may become present well before birth. It is necessary to have this bond whether psychological as in the case of adoptive or gay and lesbian "mothers" or birth mothers. It stimulates mothers to focus entirely on their newborn infants. The infant must have the total attention of their mothers early on in order to thrive and feel loved. Some mothers report experiencing a psychic energetic bond with their child even if they are not in close proximity, sensing if they are hungry, in pain, or in danger. Adoptive mothers and gay and lesbian parents report feeling the same bond. Differentiation proceeds the same way in adoptive families. The description of "mothering" can apply to anyone who accepts the mothering role.

When mothers give birth to their children, the birth separates the baby from his or her mother, giving them the physical space to continue to grow physically into adulthood. This is a physical differentiation. It is as important for both the mother and child to begin to slowly separate emotionally as well, providing the space for the child to grow emotionally. Mother and child must separate or differentiate slowly in the best way for both as the child grows in order to let them discover who they really are as the child grows into adulthood and the mother into maturity. During this slow differentiation, conflicts arise and need to be resolved. This is a process that is normal, necessary and healthy. Adoptive families go through the same process as do lesbian and gay parented families. Lesbian and gay parented families may have different family constellations, but the issues are the same. Their children have been planned for and care has been taken to negotiate who will do what to provide for the child's needs. Their roles are clear to their children from the beginning. Research has shown that these children thrive and do well. They are loved and know it. Most gay and lesbian families are good enough or better.

Emotional bonds will always exist between parents and children. Love will always be there and be most profound when parents and children fully accept each other for who they really are.

Differentiation is normal. Much of the conflict between child and parent involving blame upon mothers is a way children may disengage or separate in order to grow. Since the infant relies upon the mother for food and sustenance he or she is normally egocentric or self-centered and is unable to have empathy for their mother. This results in an inability to understand that their mother is a separate person with her own life. Any lack of sensitivity to the child's needs may be perceived by the child as rejection or lack of love. Of course good enough mothers are not perfect and children must develop an awareness of and empathy for their mother. This is what happened to my daughter when she was not carpooled. She felt unloved. At the time that happened, I was in the final crunch of writing my dissertation, and she was not able to empathize. I was so busy; I was insensitive to her needs.

In today's world, most mothers work and must have separate lives, apart from their children. Society has changed in major ways. The rise of single parent homes, mostly run by mothers, the need for more money to support a family as the economy has changed, technological growth, and feminism. There is societal pressure to conform and become a "consumer". Technological growth has a huge influence on everyone and the most impact on children. It can produce a profound negative impact on children. This will be discussed at length in chapter six.

Mothers must become more differentiated from their children than mothers from previous generations. Fathers are increasingly called upon to be more closely bonded than ever before. The resulting increased differentiation of mothers from their infants is necessary for survival in these times. However, it can cause misunderstandings, no matter how much children and parents love each other, setting the stage for possible mother bashing at a later time.

## Challenges in the Process of Differentiation

Challenges in the differentiation process are varied. Some mothers have difficulty letting their children differentiate from them. This type of mother often has fewer interests outside her home and has devoted her life to being a "good mother". Lack of involvement with other life interests that captivate and excite her may cause her to continue to focus all her attention on her children, longer than is healthy for both mother and child. She may be fearful of losing her only identity, that of "mom".

A mother's inability to allow differentiation may either cause a child to rebel and reject their mother, or to remain undifferentiated and therefore unable to grow into who they are. They sometimes maintain the same opinions and actions as their mother, even though they may go to college, leave home, marry and have their own children. Their primary bond may remain with their mother. This can cause frustration for spouses as well as their children. There are extreme cases in which the child never leaves home, may continue to be supported by his or her mother, and never marry.

I remembered my clinical case of James. James was the youngest of 5 children. The family lived on a farm. He came to therapy because he was unable to sustain a relationship with any woman and was afraid to leave his mother. He feared his mother and also said he loved her. He also mentioned that he was worried that his mother would not survive without him. James wanted to leave, but thought he could not make it alone, off the farm Every time he became involved with a woman he thought he loved, he brought her home to meet his mother. During therapy he realized that his mother had undermined all his relationships by pointing out flaws in the women to him, or convincing him that she was too good for him.

When James was born, his mother, Sylvia was 45 years old. Sylvia was not close to her husband at that time and became totally absorbed in James after his birth. She took him everywhere with her and discouraged differentiation. As James grew older, Sylvia kept him close to home and discouraged socialization. Her other children were finishing high school, getting married, and leading their own lives. They were not very interested in James and may have resented all the attention Sylvia gave him. James was extremely gifted with a genius IQ. Sylvia discouraged him from going to college by convincing him he did not need that, as someday he would inherit the farm. After high school James tried to escape his mother by joining the Army. Sylvia applied to the army for a Hardship Discharge and He was given an Honorable Hardship Discharge and ordered home. Sylvia convinced him the Army was too difficult for him and suggested that

39

he might get a bad back from all the exertion required of him. She convinced him he should stay with her and she would always take care of him. Soon after he returned from the Army James's father died suddenly of a heart attack. James then felt his mother really needed him and he couldn't leave home.

The outcome of therapy was that James realized his dilemma, became more aware of who he was and what he wanted. He maintained a good relationship with his mother, but stopped sharing everything with her. He finally met the woman of his dreams, got engaged, and set a wedding date before introducing her to his mother. That was very courageous for him. James introduced his fiancée to Sylvia 2 months before a planned wedding. Sylvia did not have time to create a rift between the two and joined in the marriage ceremony. He and his new bride, Anne left the farm and moved out of state. James was 55 years old at that time.

There are also children who fear differentiating from their mothers, even though their mother wishes for this. They may fear making their own decisions, finding out who they really are and living an independent life. This may be the result of early life experiences resulting in low self-esteem or a heredity trait.

I worked with another clinical case where Linda, the mother, was the child of a mother who differentiated from her before she was ready. Her mother was a high powered attorney in a prestigious law firm in the town where they lived. Linda felt unloved and as a result developed low self-esteem. She had difficulty in school and did not perform as well as her siblings. Linda felt angry at her mother and did not know why. She refused to go to college after finishing high school and decided to marry so she could fulfill her only dream, to be a "perfect mother", she came in for counseling when her oldest child, a college graduate, refused to do what she demanded and married a woman she was sure would ruin him. Her son refused to have anything more to do with her. She was devastated. Her other son and daughter did whatever she asked and she was very proud of them. She had become a mother who could not let her children differentiate. Her awareness of the dynamics of her situation helped her allow her older son and daughter the freedom to be different from her. Her oldest son continues his refusal to communicate with her.

Another challenge to this process is when a mother must differentiate too quickly for her child. Since most children need the total absorption of their mother for their first few years, this can be problematic. Awareness of possible problems is the first step in preventing difficulties. If a partner, relative or friend can help fill in the gaps with communication of love and explanations of the need to be away can support the child to feel loved by their mother, This mother can still be a good enough mother.

Some groups have practiced what is called multimatric mothering. This means parenting a child by "many mothers". An interesting example of this may be found in Israeli Kibbutzim (plural). A kibbutz is essentially a type of commune, developed in Israel in the mid-1950s. Kibbutzim were based on utopian ideals with hopes that mothers could be freed from child care and have time to apply themselves to other work. The children would benefit from learning equality and group consciousness. The education authority of the kibbutz was responsible for the rearing and wellbeing of the children born on the kibbutz. The kibbutz took care of their food, clothing and medical treatment. Originally the children were separated from their mothers shortly after birth, and could only spend several hours a day with their parents. The children slept in their nurseries and became bonded with not only their own parents, but with their caretakers. This extreme separation became uncomfortable for both parents and children. The process gradually evolved over the years until the children were spending more and more time with their parents and were only gone during the day. Kibbutzim involvement with child-raising eventually died out by the 1980's.

A lot was learned by this social experiment. Children who did not sleep at home had some problems with attachment. However, the results of having many mothers were essentially positive after the children began staying home with their families at night. Families became more important again and most children then benefitted from having also bonded with other mothers outside the family. Positive effects also depended on the personalities of each individual child. Analyzing this process supports the belief that children can thrive with more than one mother.

As I mentioned earlier, every child is different from every other child, as is every mother different from every other mother. There are differences in personality, abilities, interests, temperament. Some are shy, others outgoing. These differences are present from birth. They can be modified by environment. It is important for both mothers and fathers to consider and accept these differences as they deal with differentiation issues.

Differentiation is healthy. Growing awareness of this process enables us to design ways to cope with this process in as healthy ways. Difficulties with differentiation explain many of the problems mothers and children have with each other. Disagreement, rebellion and conflict are major symptoms. Since parents are responsible for the socialization of their children, it is imperative that they continue to teach them appropriate behavior, values, and empathy as well as enforcing family rules with consistency.

Everyone accepts the "terrible twos" as a normal developmental milestone that is necessary for a growing toddler in order to learn who they are, that they are separate from their mother, and can assert themselves. There is no blame. This is instead, a milestone, marking the beginning of differentiation. Later differentiation must also not include blame in order to accomplish it. The two year old is supported in their awareness of separateness while still being guided and taught the values and rules of the family and society with consistent discipline as necessary. The teenager must be supported and taught with continued appropriate consistent rules until they reach maturity.

I was reminded of one of my clinical cases involving Susan and her 21 year old son, Fred. Fred was the one who asked for help with Susan, his mother. He had finished his senior year in college and was in the Navy. He did not like to visit his parents because he said they tried to control him. He described his mother as continuing to set deadlines as to when he should come home and who he should date. She also insisted he go to church with the family, even though he did not wish to do so. She tried to pick out his girlfriends. The crisis occurred when he met and fell in love with Cindy, who had been in basic training with him in the Navy. When he brought her home to meet his parents, his mother immediately began to show Cindy pictures of Fred's old girlfriends and tell her of negative things that had happened to Fred in his past. When Fred and Cindy said they did not want to go to church on Sunday morning, both Susan and her husband Tom ordered them to leave the house. Fred and Cindy left and were both hurt and upset about the situation. They decided to cut off contact with Fred's mother. A short time later, they began living together and became engaged. A year later they decided to contact Fred's parents and told Susan and Tom of the wedding they planned. They asked for help with addresses for the guest list and attempted to introduce Tom and Susan to Cindy's parents. Susan refused to get the address list to Cindy's mother to help with the wedding arrangements or make any overtures of friendship to help with the wedding plans. She also refused to come to counseling to help resolve the situation. Fred dealt with feelings of betrayal and anger; He decided to separate from his parents.

What happened between Fred and Susan was an extreme example of Susan's inability to allow her children to differentiate from her. We have discussed the importance of differentiation, defined individuation, and looked at examples of some of the pitfalls that are possible. You may wonder how this enables mothers to take themselves off the hot seat. It provides an understanding of some of the dynamics that occur between mother and child and illustrates the concepts of differentiation and individuation more clearly. If mothers can understand and accept that differentiation and individuation are normal, they can avoid blaming themselves when their adult children occasionally criticize them.

## Positive effects of Differentiation

I agree with Freud's belief that freeing an individual from the authority of his parents is one of the most needed, but painful processes brought about by normal development. Freud stated in his book, *The Sexual Enlightenment of Children (1905)*, that, "...the whole progress of society rests upon the opposition between successive generations". Mothers can stop blaming themselves for children who differentiate and individuate in ways they may not understand. The world needs them, especially now with the rapid changes occurring in society and technology. An interesting behavior that reportedly occurs after children reach maturity is how they relate to their mothers after they become adults. The question becomes, "Are they able to see the real you?"

Something I always wished for and visualized is that after my children grew up they would see beyond my role in their life as "mother" and into the heart of who I really am as a person. This does not occur in most cases. Both children and mothers view each other within their role-relationship to each other. When a child comes home for a visit, they automatically expect to be nurtured in ways similar to the ways they were treated as a child. Their very presence triggers the nurturer behavior within the mother.

A psychologist friend once told me that he visited his mother once a year and that it was emotionally difficult. He described his feelings on these visits and said when he started his trip, he felt himself getting "younger and younger", until when he walked up his mother's sidewalk, he felt 10 years old. When his mother opened the door, he actually experienced himself as looking up to her. (The reality was that he was taller than she was.)

My mother was very nurturing. As she aged, she reached a time in her life when she could no longer give, only receive. I remember feeling a deep sadness when I realized she could no longer nurture me. It is very difficult if not impossible to transcend the role expectations we have for our mothers. Most often, we cannot really understand who our parent was, until they are gone.

When I thought of my feelings toward my adult children when they come to visit, I sometimes find myself recreating something from their childhood. Perhaps fixing a favorite meal, or arranging something they might enjoy similar to something from their past.

Even though I visualize myself talking to them adult to adult, we both gravitate toward "mother" and "child". This is a normal phenomenon, inherent in parent child relationships.

Signs of maturity for the child occur when he or she is able to function independently in society, knows who they are and can ask a parent's opinion about something, hear the response, consider it, and respond the same way they would to any other person of maturity. A sign of complete differentiation of the mother from her child would be to respond the same way they would to a peer, to truly hear their child's ideas, give their opinion, and gracefully accept a disagreement in the same way they would with a beloved friend. I began to feel better as I continued to search for ways to understand what had happened to me and many other mothers I know.

The next issue I wondered about was the effects of single parenting upon both the relationships between mothers and their children and possible harm to both of them.

# Chapter 3

# SINGLE MOTHERS

*Alone*

*Alone on an island with you my love*
*Feeling scared, can I do this?*
*And loving you so*
*The twisting and turning, resenting and yearning*
*So fearing, but freeing*
*And loving you so*
*The running and working, the feeding and playing*
*But growing and learning*
*And loving you so*
*The teaching and hoping, the caring and coping*
*With joy and commitment*
*And loving you so*
*We'll do it together forever and ever*
*While loving you so*

When I was a professor at the University of Wisconsin some years ago, I was teaching a class in the School of Nursing and had several female students in the class who were single parents, struggling to parent their children and get through school so they could make enough money to give their children a good life. I had grown up in a privileged home and had been taught that everyone is responsible for whatever happens to them and one should help people, but never give them money as that would encourage irresponsibility.

One afternoon I was sitting in my office organizing the next day's schedule when there was a knock at the door. Anne, one of the single parent students was at my door looking very upset. I invited her to come in and tell me what was wrong. She burst into tears and told me I was her last resort. She had a six year old daughter at home and had run out of money due to the cost of an antibiotic to help her daughter. Her scholarship money had not come in on time and she had no money for food and didn't know what to do. She asked for my help. My heart was touched. I believed her. I felt tears coming to my eyes and held them back. Part of me said to myself. This could be a con. Don't ever give money to someone. It will make them irresponsible and think you are a "soft touch". I couldn't reject her request. I believe I reached into my purse and gave her a $20.00 bill. Anne looked so relieved, she sobbed her thanks to me and said she would pay me back, after which she ran out my door. Over the next semester she would show up at my office and give me a dollar or two, until she had indeed paid her debt. Since she was no longer in my class, I did not see her for a long while. Two years later she again showed up at my office to tell me she had graduated and that the $20.00 had been a turning point for her. She had been ready to drop out of school if she could not afford to put food on the table for her daughter that night. I learned a lot from her. She was certainly a good enough mother. Census Bureau statistics indicate that today 50% of U.S. children will spend some part of their childhoods in a single parent family. In the 1950's, 60% of U.S families consisted of two married parents: a breadwinner and a homemaker. Today only 20 percent of American children live in such a family. Instead, couples' divorce, or never marry in the first place, and may form new households.

Most single mothers experience many more stresses than their partnered counterparts and some of them feel constant regret for their inability to be "perfect". They often must cope with different problems than those of mothers who are not alone.

## Facts about Single Parenting

Custodial mothers in single parent homes are in a unique situation today to be easy targets for Mother Bashing. There are many false assumptions about them. Most of them are hardworking, dedicated women who love their children dearly and are good enough mothers or better. However, there is a high risk of poverty and all the stresses that are present with poverty can effect a child's development negatively. It is difficult to be a good enough mother under these conditions.

The categorization of almost all single mothers as "welfare mother deadbeats who are milking the system for money because they are too lazy to work" may have had some truth to it in the past, but it is far from appropriate at this time. It is extremely challenging and stressful for single mothers to be good enough mothers at this time.

According to the United States recent Census Bureau reports (2011), there are approximately 14.4 million single parents in the United States today and those parents are responsible for raising 23.4 million children. Approximately 81.7 % of custodial parents are mothers.

The assumption that most single mothers were single from the outset is false. Those divorced or separated number 43.5%. Those who have never been married number 37.1%, married-18.3% and, 1.1% were widowed. Another assumption about single mothers is that most are unemployed. Again, this is not true. Gainfully employed single mothers' number 76%. Poverty is not the norm for most single parent families. However, custodial single mothers and their children are twice as likely to live in poverty as the general population. Another false assumption about single mothers is that most receive government assistance. Only 42.9% received some form of government assistance. They are not all young. Custodial mothers 40 years of age or older number 39.1 percent. Over half of them are raising only one child. There are many single parents who are dedicated mothers working hard to create a positive life for their children and themselves. These courageous mothers in the world do not belong on the hot seat! Society often places them there. Social Change is the primary cause for dilemmas of the single mother.

## Stressors faced by Single Parent Families

Some of the stressors faced by single parent families are: visitation and custody problems, the effects of continuing conflict between the parents, less opportunity for parents and children to spend time together, effects of the breakup on children's school performance and peer relations, disruptions of extended family relationships, problems that may be caused by the parent's dating and entering new relationships and, the effects of poverty.

Single parents are more likely to be raising their children in poverty than the general population.

The effects of a single-parent home on a child's behavior can have far reaching effects that may impact several areas of their lives. These include academic achievement and social behaviors.

Academic achievement is affected by low income. The mother must spend more time working to support the child and has less time to spend with their child. The mothers may not be as available to help with homework.

Having only one income earner in the home puts single parent households at risk for poverty. Living in poverty is stressful and can elicit emotional effects in children. These may include low self-esteem, increased anger and frustration with an increased risk for violent behavior. In single parent homes when the father is not available, there may be feeling of abandonment, sadness, loneliness and difficulty socializing and connecting with others.

The negative effects of a single parent home vary. Some single parent homes are led by professional mothers who never married and chose to adopt a child. Others are widowed women with adequate financial resources to stay at home. Parenting styles are critical. The personality and age of the child is an important variable. I spoke with women who never wished to marry, but wanted a child. One in particular that I remember was a physician who purposefully got pregnant and had a little girl. The child was well loved and grew up to become a physician also.

Poverty seems to produce the most negative and profound effects upon the single parent children. Those living in poverty may also have to live in a neighborhood with high crime rates. These neighborhoods are rampant with negative influences on children.

Mothers with higher educational levels can usually get higher paying jobs that can remove some of their stress. Stress levels upon single mothers who are not able to earn a livable income are higher. The more stressed the single mother becomes; the harder it is for her to be a good enough mother.

## Positive Effects of Single Parenting

The positive effects of single parenting depend upon such factors as personality types and parenting techniques. There was a study at Cornell University showing that positive single parenting did not have any negative impact on the social and educational development of the 12 and 13 year old children they evaluated. They found the children exhibited strong responsibility skills because they were often called upon to help out more with family chores and tasks. The children formed close bonds with their parent as they were closely dependent on each other throughout the child ' s life. Some of the children also formed closer bonds with extended family members or family friends than they may have in an intact family. I have personally known several cases of very successful parenting by single mothers that turned out well adjusted, happy adults.

The following is an interesting true story to consider:

There was a single mother living in England who had been divorced from an abusive husband. He paid no child support. She had become a single mother and was unable to get a job that could support her and provide daycare for her infant daughter. So, it was painfully necessary to apply for welfare. The money she received was just enough to pay for food and a small apartment. This mother struggled for several years to survive. She had several close friends who were emotionally supportive. This mother spent every day with her daughter and showered her with love. While her daughter slept, she decided to write a book. The book she wrote was later published. It was the first Harry Potter book. The woman's name was JK Rowling.

The next question that needed to be examined further was, "What causes adult children of good enough mothers in any of the family constellations to blame their mothers?" It may be the result problems with memory.

# Chapter 4

# MEMORY

*Reality*

*Forgetting to remember and Remembering to forget*
*Obfuscates the problem, to find the real truth*
*Forgetting to remember and Remembering to forget*
*Calms the fears and stop the tears*
*But blocks the real truth*
*Forgetting to remember and Remembering to forget*
*Can hurt and harm or help confirm for what we yearn*
*To believe our truth is real*

M emory is an elusive thing. Children and their parents quite often remember things differently. I remember when my daughter told me our house was always messy and she always kept her room neat. She stated that she always made her bed every day. Well, I remembered that we had a housekeeper at the time who kept the house immaculate and that she kept her room a mess and seldom made her bed unless the housekeeper was planning to clean her room that day. (We had a rule in our house that unless you picked up your room, you would have to make your own bed and dust.) A number of the mothers and children I surveyed mentioned that they remembered things differently.

As I recalled the differences between my memories and my daughters, I wondered at the differences in our perceptions of the past. As a psychologist, I had long been concerned with memory as some of my clients had retrieved memories of terrible child abuse that included torture, satanic cult abuse, sexual abuse, emotional abuse, and physical abuse. I had helped many trauma victims who reported suddenly remembering traumatic events that seemed to have been "repressed", about terrible things that happened to them in the past. It was considered appropriate in the 1980s to accept repressed memories and even search for them to help victims recover. I was always concerned about the validity of these memories until they were corroborated by others or factual information of some kind.

It is important for mothers and children to understand the fallibility of memory as related to past events in order to avoid blaming yourself or someone else for anything. Things your children remember as well as what you remember may be skewed to meet our needs in the here and now.

## Dissociated Memory

My first case related to a certain type of repressed memory or dissociated memory that happened in the early 80s. I had been working with a young woman, Ellen, who had been depressed. At one point she was so depressed, I feared she might take her life and arranged for her to be hospitalized. During her hospitalization, Ellen had suddenly exhibited great rage, picked up a hospital bed, and reportedly threw it against the wall. After this she felt much better and was discharged. I worked with her for over a year, spending a lot of time discussing her feelings in the present and upsets about the past. She was able to work as a secretary and attended college part time. Ellen did make improvements in therapy, but still experienced depression. I was beginning to think therapy was not the only answer to help her and she might need an antidepressant, then something strange happened.

It was a cold and blustery day when Ellen entered my office and sat on my couch. I was across from her in an easy chair. Within five minutes after our greetings, she started to sob. I questioned her as to what was wrong. Ellen continued to sob hysterically. I grabbed a Kleenex box, crossed the room, and sat next to her. She never said a word, only sobbed and sobbed hysterically. This went on for about 30 minutes. I handed her Kleenex after Kleenex. Her face was covered with tears and her eye makeup had run, creating dark rivulets of moisture over her cheeks. She had used up an entire box of Kleenex which was filled with her tears and crumpled in her lap.

Suddenly Ellen stopped crying, turned, looked at me, and said in a cold voice, "What are you doing over here?" I said, "I came over here to comfort you while you were crying." She responded, "I wasn't crying." I assured her she was and when she continued to deny this, I asked her to look at all the Kleenexes in her lap and on the floor. I also told her that her tears were still wet on her face. Ellen felt her tears with her fingers and looked in a mirror. Her eyes widened and she got a shocked look on her face. She then said "Oh my God, All I remember was you were over there (pointing to the easy chair) and I was over here and then suddenly you are over here. She then looked her watch and realized that 45 minutes had passed and she did not remember anything. We were both stunned.

I didn't know how to explain to myself what had happened. Why didn't she remember what had happened? Why was she crying? So I decided to consult with a colleague who was a psychiatrist to get advice about how to proceed. My psychiatrist friend said he didn't know either, but gave me a journal to read about dissociative disorders. I had heard of this, but tended to disbelieve dissociative disorders really existed. I called several other colleagues, but none knew any more than I did. I somehow found information about a meeting coming up in Chicago about Dissociation, and decided to attend. That marked the beginning of a long career working with trauma victims. Ellen was subsequently diagnosed with a major dissociative disorder. Her memory for the time in my office and other memories from her childhood had been "dissociated." You will read more about her case in the chapter on child abuse.

Dissociation means to cut off part of yourself from other parts of yourself. What does that have to do with Mother blaming? I wondered about my daughter's negative recollections of her childhood. They were not dissociated. I believed it only fair to question my memory of events also which were not dissociated. Dissociated memory loss is related to early childhood trauma. In this case it was later clear that the trauma had nothing to do with her mother. Her mother was a good enough mother.

During the 1990s many parents were accused of horrific abuses by adult children who claimed their memories had been repressed. Some of the children had recovered their memories in therapy. Suddenly, many therapists were accused of implanting false memories through the use of hypnosis and suggestion. I became very concerned about these issues and questioned the validity of all recovered memories unless they were corroborated in some clear way. Many of them were validated and it was not possible to validate or invalidate others.

A group of parents who believed they had been falsely accused by their adult children of child abuse formed the False Memory Syndrome Foundation in 1992. They labeled inaccurate memories as a "False Memory Syndrome". When I read about this group, I became very concerned about the possibility of inadvertently creating a false memory in my work with Trauma victims so I decided to attend their first meeting. I wanted to learn more so I could better avoid suggesting a false memory to my patients. I looked forward to a scientific discussion about this issue at the meeting.

I had difficulty registering. When I requested a registration form, I was unable to obtain it. After 3 or 4 attempts, I began to wonder if they did not want therapists to attend. I decided to request a registration form using my husband's last name. They sent it immediately. I did go to the meeting and discovered it was not a scientific discussion, but appeared to be an organizational meeting, only dealing with research that supported their viewpoint. They refused to discuss the possibility of any truth in memories that had not always been remembered. When they discovered I was a psychologist and worked with trauma victims, they asked me to leave.

I was surprised at their response to me and became concerned for clients I knew, who remembered traumatic events belatedly that had been corroborated as well as those who may have had inaccurate memories inadvertently suggested to them by well-meaning therapists.

## Spontaneous Remembering of Dissociated Memory

I will never forget Harry. Harry was referred to me by his girlfriend. He was very depressed and his girlfriend was concerned that he might kill himself. I agreed to see him if he wanted to come, and finally one afternoon he called for an appointment. When he arrived he sat on the edge of his chair and looked at me warily. All he would tell me is that he should be dead and felt worthless. It took about 10 sessions to begin to connect with him. All I could do is try to establish trust and help him look at himself more positively. My heart went out to him. I could feel his pain. His eyes were so sad and he seemed fearful. As the weeks went by Harry seemed more comfortable with me and finally one day he said, "I have something to give you." He pulled out a gun and handed it to me. I felt shaken, but accepted the gun and placed it in my locked filing cabinet. He told me he had been keeping it so he could kill himself when he felt ready. Harry then said, "I will tell you why I am so upset."

He told me that starting the year before; he had begun having memories of some terrible things that had happened in his childhood. They intruded upon his waking life and also kept him from sleeping. He had believed he could tell no one. Harry also said he had rage deep within him and was afraid he might hurt someone. I asked for assurance that I would be safe with him. He said he would not hurt me and I believed him.

Harry told me that it all began when he was an altar boy in the Catholic Church. The priest had sexually abused him in many ways. He was threatened with death and damnation if he would ever tell anyone. His faith in God was shattered. As he grew up, he forgot about what had happened, but had always refused to go to church with his family and had trouble relating to other children as well as his family, who were devoted Catholics and active in their church, the same church with the abusive priest still there who had abused him.

I helped him process the events and he appeared to come to terms with what had happened. However, one night he called me at home and told me he was going to kill the priest. I, of course, called the police who warned the priest and took him to another location. Harry later told me he was glad I had prevented the murder.

We soon found out that the same priest had abused other little boys. Harry got a lawyer and tried to get some restitution from the church. The church did pay for some of his therapy later, but a local Judge ruled that there could be no legal case because his memories had been delayed and the statute of limitations was in effect. The judge also mentioned the inaccuracy of delayed memory.

Harry became depressed at this outcome. He needed to be validated by the church in order to recover. I worked with Harry's family to help them accept Harry's accusations of priest abuse. Harry became functional and attended medical school to become a physician.. He decided to terminate therapy for a time. I believed he still harbored feelings he had not dealt with and suggested we continue, but he insisted he must go on with his life.

A year after he terminated therapy, I decided to move to another state. I sent him referrals to other therapists, should he need therapy again. Harry came in for one last visit to say goodbye.

The story of Harry does not have a happy ending. Several years ago, about 5 years after I moved to Santa Fe, New Mexico, I received a long distance call from Harry's sister. She told me Harry had been found dead from a drug overdose. He never asked me to give his gun back.

This all occurred during the time of the False Memory Syndrome popularity. Any delayed memories were blamed on therapist suggestion. I knew I had suggested nothing. He had his memories when I met him and they were delayed as well as corroborated by the reports of other children. Society failed him and the church failed him.

There are false memories and there are true delayed memories. The only way to be sure about which is which is by corroboration.

The advent of the False Memory Syndrome Foundation was the beginning of bitter division within psychology and psychiatry. Families were divided and many therapists were sued for "implanting false memories". A positive outcome was increased research in studies on suggestibility.

I became determined to find the truth and opened my mind to all possibilities. As I looked back on this experience, I realized it is relevant to mother bashing. I began to empathize with mothers who have been falsely accused as I believed I had been by my daughter, even though there was no child abuse involved. Mother blaming of good enough mothers is the focus of this book. Harry had a good enough mother who was not in any way responsible for his problems.

## Seven Ways We Distort Memory

Daniel Schacter's book, "The Seven Sins of Memory"(2001), which was first published in 1997, provides information about the most recent research that helps us understand what really may be going on when people remember things differently. Schacter describes the seven ways we distort memory. The following include paraphrasing his information interspersed with my comments.

The first way memory becomes distorted is by the passage of time. Research shows us that as people get older, they do not remember things as well from the past. This forgetting, if severe, may be related to Alzheimer's disease. I remember meeting a friend's aged mother who had Alzheimer's. We met in a restaurant. When I was introduced to her, she and I talked for about 15 minutes. She seemed interested in my work and excited about going to lunch with me and her son. I left the table for 5 minutes to answer a phone call. When I returned she said. "I don't believe I know you" Her son explained to her that we had just met. No amount of prompting or cueing could bring forth her memory. This type of memory distortion is not relevant to mother bashing.

The second way memory becomes distorted is due to lack of attention or absent mindedness. Lapses of attention that cause failure to remember information that was either never perceived or overlooked. It is extremely common for multitasking people to forget or distort reality in this way. An example of this would be a woman puts her watch down on the edge of a couch. Several minutes later she can't remember where she put it and spends an hour looking for it. This type of memory distortion is also not usually present in mother bashing.

The third way memory becomes distorted is by blocking information that feels like it is on the tip of your tongue or information of a traumatic nature which may have been dissociated. The former is a familiar but frustrating experience most people have to some degree when we can't seem to remember information we know that we know. Sometimes the blocking experience is mildly irritating, but at other times it can cause us great anxiety. I have had the embarrassing experience of being at a party and seeing a woman I knew well who I wanted to introduce to another person. Suddenly, I couldn't remember her name. Fortunately, she came forward and introduced herself. Though blocking on names of familiar acquaintances can be sometimes embarrassing, most people manage to retrieve the information successfully at a later time. This type of memory distortion can occur at a deeper level, because the mind does not want to remember a traumatic event. It could be present in child abuse situations. You will read more about this type of memory distortion in the chapter on child abuse.

The fourth way memory may become distorted is by assigning memory to the wrong source. It is a form of misattribution. Misattribution can happen in eye witness testimony. For example, the wrong person may be identified as the guilty culprit in a bank robbery, when the person identified could actually be someone the witness saw the day before in a grocery store. Many instances of eyewitness misidentification have been documented. People often have sketchy recollections of the precise details of a previous experience. This distortion is usually not present in mother blaming.

An example of misattribution occurred in the failed search for "John Doe 2" in the Oklahoma City bombing of 1995. Timothy McVeigh was apprehended as the culprit shortly after the bombing in April, 1995. At the same time, the FBI began a nationwide manhunt for a second suspect they believed had accompanied McVeigh when he rented a van from a body shop in Junction City, Kansas, 2 days before the bombing. Witnesses generated an artist's sketch of the alleged accomplice which appeared on television and was featured in newspapers around the country. It was later proved there was no accomplice.

Even though one eyewitness testified that there was only one person who rented McVeigh's van, another witness "remembered" there were two persons who rented it. The source of that memory turned out to be attributed to an unrelated visit to the rental facility a day after the bombing, when an army Sergeant and his friend also rented a van in that witness's presence. His description of that second person exactly matched the person in the unrelated rental. This type of memory distortion is not usually present in mother bashing.

The fifth way memory may be distorted is based more on how we feel now than what happened then. We are biased to rescript our memories to fit with our present views and needs. There may be distorting influences of our present knowledge, beliefs, and feelings on new experiences or our later memories of them. The way we were depends upon the way we are. This type of distortion may occur when we avoid taking responsibility for our current problems. It is relevant to mother bashing.

When patients afflicted by chronic physical pain are experiencing high levels of pain in the present, they are biased to recall similarly high levels of pain in the past. When their pain in the present is minor, past pain becomes minor too in their memories. This is true for emotional pain also.

This type of biased memory distortion helps those who use it feel consistent with their reality of the present. It reduces the emotional discomfort that could result from conflicting thoughts and feelings. An example would be a young adult who remembered her mother depriving her of her allowance in high school because she was suffering the current effects of losing her job in the present. This type of memory distortion is often found in mother blaming.

The sixth way memory may be distorted is based upon inaccurate suggestions by others. Suggestibility in memory refers to an individual's tendency to incorporate misleading information from external sources. These may include other people, written materials, pictures, or the media. It is somewhat related to misattribution in the sense that the conversion of suggestions into inaccurate memories must involve misattribution. Some people are more suggestible than others. Knowledge of suggestibility in memory distortion is extremely important to therapists working with trauma victims. Therapists must receive dissociated memories with great care and avoid suggestion. I have experienced several cases that I hoped were not true memories. One of them involved a woman who was brought to me by her therapist for consultation. This type of memory distortion could be present in mother bashing.

Andrea was a small, mild, sweet looking woman in her 30's. She was single and worked in a preschool. She had a history of depression, dissociation, and difficulty in personal relationships. A few weeks before I saw her, her therapist reported that she had dissociated during a therapy session and shared that she had been abused by a satanic cult as a child and had the "devil" within her. Her therapist stated that during one session she had taken on the "characteristics of the Devil and stated that was who she was". After that episode in his office, she claimed to have had no memory of the satanic cult or of becoming the Devil.

During my consultation with her, I took her history and asked her what she would like to accomplish during our time together. She stated that she had been told by her therapist all that had occurred about the cult and the devil and that she wanted to find out if it was true. She was concerned that she might be a danger to the children at the preschool where she worked. She had worked there for 10 years and was beloved by all.

I asked for her permission to talk with the 2 parts of her that her therapist had described. She agreed. What happened next, I will never forget. All it took to elicit the part of Andrea who" knew about the satanic cult abuse" was to ask Andrea to close her eyes and ask the part of Andrea who knew about the abuse to come forward. Andrea shifted her body and opened her eyes. She no longer looked sweet and mild. She sat up straight and tall in her chair and had a somewhat angry look on her face. I asked her to tell me about what had happened to Andrea when she was a child. She told me details of torture, sexual abuse, and human sacrifice. There were no suggestions given by me. When she was finished, I thanked her for the information, asked her to close her eyes, and requested to talk with the part of her that "thought" she was the Devil.

I was not prepared for what happened next. When Andrea opened her eyes, she looked entirely different; nothing like the Andrea who had come into my office. Her eyes appeared narrower and darker. Her face somehow looked narrow where previously it was rounded. Andrea also seemed much larger than before. Her expression was one of rage.

At first she began to sniff the air as she looked around my office. When she looked into my eyes, I shuddered at the darkness I saw there. I felt like I was part of the movie, "The Exorcist". When I asked her who she was, she said "Satan" in a deep hoarse voice. I felt shock, but went into my "calm therapeutic mode". I told her she was not Satan, but only thought she was. I believed this was true.

Andrea maintained this identity for about 15 minutes. Toward the end of the 15 minutes she seemed to be less adamant about being Satan. When I asked her to close her eyes and let me talk to the Andrea who had come into my office, she did. I must admit I kept my fingers crossed that I would be able to access the sweet little lady who entered the office.

Andrea said she did not remember anything about the other parts of herself. I explained what had happened in detail and showed her a video recording of the session.

After Andrea left, I realized I had been somewhat shocked by her revelations. I felt shaky and tearful. After I shed a few tears, I decided I needed to debrief with a colleague as soon as possible. One of the other psychologists in my office was able to help me stabilize. That night I was plagued by nightmares related some of the graphic details she had shared. It took me several days to feel stabilized. After this experience I decided to avoid future cases involving cult abuse, real or suggested. Before this experience, I believed I could handle with equanimity anything anyone could tell me.

My questions about this case were: Could it be true? Was it suggested? How? Why, and by whom? And most importantly what should be done?

At that time there were many reports of Satanic Cult Abuse. Everyone in the therapeutic community was not only very concerned, but traumatized by some of the things we were hearing from patients. I always wondered if it could be true. There were many descriptions in the media about Satanic Cult Abuse at that time. Therapists could not negate these reports as their job is to listen to whatever the client wants to discuss. Perhaps some therapists inadvertently suggested these memories. They could also have been suggested by the media coverage or hearing about satanic cult abuse from others. Dissociative patients are highly suggestible.

I gave her therapist the videotape and recommended that Andrea stop working with children for the time being. We also discussed ways to proceed therapeutically and to report Andrea's revelations to law enforcement. At that time there was a special police unit dedicated to the investigation of satanic cult abuse.

I heard later that the police found no evidence of Cult activity related to Andrea. There was a high probability that her revelations were the result of suggestion. I never knew for sure.

The seventh way memory may be distorted is by a repeated recall of disturbing information or events. This may be labeled the persistence of memory. It is probably the most debilitating memory distortion of all. Persistence of memory involves remembering those things you wish you could forget. Sometimes the result is only mildly irritating, such as having a familiar tune go through your head over and over. Emotional events are more easily placed in the "persistent category."

Sometimes remembering an event over and over is a way to think over what could have been done differently. A mild example of persistence of memory occurred when my husband inadvertently backed into his son's car as it was parked in back of the garage door. Both cars were damaged. Both he and his son thought about the incident over and over in order to figure out what each of them could have done differently. His son berated himself for parking there in the first place. My husband berated himself for not being careful enough and also not telling his son to move the car. This mild case of memory persistence lasted for several days, but resulted in both of them avoiding an accident like that again. This level of memory persistence can be productive.

Higher levels of memory persistence can last for years or decades and may be extremely hurtful. Terror in the past is related to both visual and auditory memories. War veterans may experience Post Traumatic Stress Disorder. (PTSD) This may include not only intrusive memories, but flashbacks of the traumatic events which cause the veteran to actually relive them. Child victims of abuse often have not only memory persistence distortions, but experience blocking as well as dissociation.

Two of the areas mentioned above are most directly related to good enough mothers and children remembering things differently. They are Bias and Suggestibility.

Bias is based more on how we feel now than what happened then. Schacter described research regarding different types of biases. The ones that seemed most related to mother blaming after good enough mothering were consistency and change. "When patients afflicted by chronic pain are experiencing high levels of pain in the present, they are biased to recall similarly high levels of pain in the past; when present pain isn't so bad, past pain experiences seem more benign, too". "Egocentric biases illustrate the powerful role of the self in orchestrating perceptions and memories of reality." People need to remember themselves in a positive light.

Ego centric biases could explain why my daughter remembered how neat she was in childhood or I remembered how the housekeeper kept our home neat.

Consistency biases could explain how perhaps the pain of something in my adult daughter's life reminded her of the pain she felt when I told her to put on a sweater under her jacket. I better understood how these distortions could affect relationships between mothers and their children. If mothers remember things differently than their children, either one or both could be distorting reality without conscious awareness.

Delineation of the effects of various types of suggestion on memory, although not relevant to mother blaming, reaffirmed my caution in work with my patients. Memories are so easily distorted, only corroboration from others who observed what had occurred, can validate their accuracy.

I could now further remove myself from the hot seat in relationship to my daughter and also have compassion for her and myself. I wondered what pain was going on in her life at the time she told me I had ruined it?

After considering how memory distortions can affect relationships between mothers and their adult children, I turned my attention toward mothers who actually abuse their children, causing them great harm.

# Chapter 5

# CHILD ABUSE

*You wanted me to be your little girl*
*You wanted me to see you as my world*
*You wanted me to be all I could be I wanted you to open your eyes and see*

*The bruises on my arms were not love*
*The pain in my eyes was not relief*
*Blood stained the white feathers of the dove*
*And she did not mourn, but she grieved*

*My childhood was dust in the wind*
*By the time I was four*
*It was over with*
*The moment you shoved me into that door*

*But, Daddy, I am sorry*
*I am sorry I wasn't everything you wanted*
*I am sorry I made you mad*
*I am sorry for being so bad*

*I took the beatings for my brother*
*Because you didn't see he had already given up*
*I carried the burden of pain for my mother*
*Because you didn't see she was already shriveled up*

*Please God, set me free*
*Take these bruises from me*
*Please take away the breath of life*
*Oh, God let me drop this knife*

*Heaven cannot set me free*
*It is not ready for me*
*I have suffered much in this life*
*But help does not come in the form of a knife*

*I will live*
*I will breathe*
*I will stand tall*
*And for myself, I will not fall*
*(By Ally Ahrens, age 15)*

T he poem above depicts some of the suffering experienced by child abuse victims. It is important for all mothers to be aware of such suffering and its causes. Good enough mothers do not abuse their children even though we may feel like it on occasion.

I spoke with five women in my pilot study who had made the decision never to have children. Two of them had been abused in childhood and did not believe they could be a good mother, because they did not know how, or might also abuse their child if they had one. Both had been trying to forgive their own mothers for years.

Some mothers unfortunately, must accept the fact that they have been abusive to their children. If that is the case, it is important for the wellbeing of their children to forgive their abusive mothers. Before forgiveness can occur, an abused child must become aware of the anger they hold and work it through. A good therapist can help as well as some of the excellent self-help books available today.

## Differences in a Child's Reaction to Child Abuse and Minor Trauma

When I compared my daughter's reaction to what I had done to upset her to the reactions of some of my patients who had endured brutal abuse such as torture, sexual abuse, and major emotional abuse, I realized the differences. A child abuse victim's reactions to their abusive parent are usually totally different from the reaction of adult children to the "minor" mistakes made by good enough mothers. Children sometimes perceive these minor mistakes as "Child Abuse". Actual child abuse victims usually do not initially blame their abuser.

It is helpful for mothers who tend to take responsibility for all their children's problems to fully understand what actual child abuse looks like. Some mothers blame themselves if their children have any difficulty whatsoever. Mothers are quite often judged and sometimes judge themselves by their child's behavior.

The seriously abused child's reaction to their parents is, for the most part, a <u>suppression</u> of anger. The child needs to believe that they are not rejected or "bad" and yearn to experience love and validation from the abusive parent. It is difficult for them to blame their parents because they need them so much. They tend to think perhaps, they caused the abuse. The event with my daughter had marked the beginning of my quest to explore and discover what was really happening between many mothers and their children. It had happened to me! My initial reaction had been to blame myself for my daughter's problems.

Years earlier I had been asked by the court to evaluate Johnny, a six year old frail looking blond boy whose father had admittedly broken his arm because he had spit out food at the table. At the time of the incident his mother took Johnny, left their home, and immediately filed for divorce. There had been many instances of beatings, torture of Johnny's pet cat that had culminated in the cat being thrown off a 4th story balcony, as well as emotional abuse, and actual physical abuse of Johnny's mother prior to the broken arm. A custody hearing was pending, awaiting my evaluation. Johnny's arm was still in a cast at the time. When I questioned Johnny about how he felt and what he thought about everything that had happened, he immediately volunteered, "I want to live with my Dad!" I was surprised and said, "Why do you want to do that?" Johnny said, "Because we do guy things together, he buys me presents and takes me to the movies." I asked him if he wasn't afraid his father might hurt him again. He smiled, and emphatically said "No!" I wondered why he wasn't afraid or angry at his father and asked, "Why aren't you afraid?" He said proudly"...because I'll never spit out food at the table again".

I realized that Johnny was incapable of understanding that parents are never supposed to physically harm them, their pets, or their mothers. He had placed the blame entirely upon himself in order to feel that he had some control of his life. He believed if he was a "good boy", then all abuse would stop. When I told him that it is not right for parents to behave this way, he got a shocked look on his face and said tearfully, "I never knew that." Ultimately the court gave full custody to Johnny's mother. This is an example of how abused children usually blame themselves first instead of their parents.

Increased awareness of child abuse may help some of us stop blaming our own mothers or feel validated in blaming them for our difficulties. If you must place your own mother on that hot seat, you might need help forgiving her. A good therapist can help.

If some readers discover they have been abusing their own children, it is important to forgive yourself, and seek help. Call a therapist or Child Protective Services in your community.

Others who read this may realize they experienced child abuse as a child. Some mothers do belong on that hot seat. If this is the case, the way to cope is to forgive and go on. A good therapist or self-help book on how to forgive can also aid you.

It is important for mothers everywhere to understand the types of hard core Child Abuse and its effects. Everyone reads about cases of horrendous abuse. The media focuses on dramatic situations that seem unbelievable. A major focus of my work as a clinical psychologist was therapy with trauma victims, many of whom were child abuse victims.

Categories of child abuse are Neglect, Physical Abuse, Sexual Abuse, and Emotional Abuse. Child Neglect is an act of omission. (Mothers are not doing something they should be doing for their children. It is a failure to provide the minimum requirements for care.) The following information about child abuse is paraphrased from the book, "Child Abuse and Neglect" (2014), by M. McCoy and M Keen.

## Neglect

Good enough mothers do not always provide "ideal" care but do meet the minimum requirements for care or better. It is generally accepted that parents are neglectful if they do not meet minimum needs for food, clothing, shelter, protection and medical care. Neglect may begin before birth. This is called "fetal neglect" which happens with drug and alcohol abuse by the mother while pregnant. Next, is postnatal exposure to drugs? (such as being exposed to a meth lab), Infants who were exposed to drugs in utero may suffer from fetal alcohol syndrome or be addicted at birth to other drugs. These drugs could affect a child's intellectual ability, ability to form relationships, a learning disability, poor impulse control, and physical problems.

A subtype of Neglect is Physical Neglect. An extreme of this, would be when a child is starved to the point of being malnourished.

In September, 2002, a couple was arrested in Tampa, Florida, and charged with maltreating a 7-year old child. The mother, Edna and her boyfriend, Sidney had locked Kimberly in her room for months and given her only minimal food and water. Kimberly, who should have weighed between 50 and 55 pounds, weighed only 29 pounds when the police found her. The room where she was kept had no mattress and Kimberly was forced to use a small closet as a bathroom. She did not attend school. Apparently, her mother occasionally tried to sneak food to her when Sidney was not around, but she said she could not leave Sidney because she had nowhere else to go.

The police learned of the case from the girl's biological father, who saw the conditions she was living in when he arrived from New York with a court order to take the child. Investigation revealed that this was not the first time the authorities had been contacted about this. The child's mother and her boyfriend had been living in New York when they came to the attention of Child Protective Services. The allegations at that time were that the child had been absent from school, and that she was not adequately supervised, and that she was medically neglected. The determination at that time was that she was "not in imminent danger".

Then in May, 2002, the family was again reported to CPS. Edna and Sidney had admitted Kimberly to a psychiatric hospital because she was having problems with incontinence. The staff at the hospital began to suspect that Kimberly was being maltreated. When Edna and Sidney realized that the hospital staff was going to report them to the state authorities, they took the child from the hospital against the doctor's orders and fled to Florida. New York social services did not contact Florida authorities to report the move because at the conclusion of their investigation in 2001 they did not think she was at a high risk and they were not able to investigate in 2002 because the family had left the state.

When Kimberly's biological father learned of her location in Florida, he obtained a court order and went to get her. Her mother handed her daughter over without conflict and Kimberly went back to New York with her father. Once in New York, Kimberly was treated for malnutrition and dehydration. It was also noted that she was bruised and had a human bite mark on her back. In addition, the doctors had to surgically remove a bead that Kimberly said the boyfriend had shoved into her ear because she was "bad". Kimberly also reported that Sidney locked her up and refused to feed her because he hated her. The detective who investigated the case reported that Sidney was jealous of the affection Edna had for Kimberly.

This is an extreme case of Abuse by neglect of Kimberly's mother. Good enough mothers may occasionally feed their child food of questionable value, but are not neglectful parents. Good enough mothers protect their children from any type of physical, sexual, or emotional abuse. Some experts consider it may be neglectful if a mother allows her child to become obese by providing only high calorie food.

As mentioned previously inadequate shelter, Inadequate supervision, exposure to domestic violence, mental health neglect (not providing recommended mental health services), educational neglect (not supporting school attendance, abandonment, and medical neglect (not providing adequate medical care) are other forms of physical neglect.

Another subtype of neglect is Emotional Neglect. Emotional neglect may be described as the failure to provide adequate affection and emotional support and permitting a child to witness domestic violence.

It is critically important that every child feel loved. We have known this for years. Psychologists have recently been studying the lasting impact of emotional neglect and have described how early deprivation of love harms children's brains. They have found that within the first 2 years of life this type of neglect may cause poor impulse control, social withdrawal, problems with coping and regulating emotions, low self-esteem, pathological behaviors such as tics, tantrums, stealing and self-punishment, poor intellectual functioning and low academic achievement.

## Physical Abuse

<u>Physical Abuse</u> is generally described as "Any non-accidental physical injury to the child, and can include striking, kicking, burning, or biting the child or any action that results in physical impairment of the child". It can cause death of the child.

You may remember the case of Johnny, whose arm was broken by his father because he spit food out at the table. Johnny's mother was a good enough mother. She immediately removed Johnny from the situation and filed for divorce. Johnny did not appreciate her actions at that time, because he believed the whole situation occurred because he was a "bad boy". It was necessary for him to have therapy after the abuse to understand it was not his fault that the violence done to him was not right. No child deserves to be treated that way no matter what they do.

## Corporal Punishment

Whenever Physical Abuse is considered, parents have questions about <u>corporal punishment</u>. The question is, "To Spank or Not to Spank? Most parents in the U.S. admit to using corporal punishment. There are reports that by the time a U.S. child is 14 years old, there is a 94% chance they have been spanked. Denmark, Austria, Finland, Germany, Iceland, Israel, Italy, Norway and Sweden have laws that forbid any corporal punishment and label it as abusive.

Different states in the U.S. take different positions about spanking. The southern states are more permissive about spanking if it is done in a reasonable manner and is moderate in degree. What was once accepted as appropriate parenting by our grandparents is now considered abusive in some states. The trend has been to avoid spanking children for the past 30 years. However I have heard more and more stories of permissive parents and out-of-control children. It is possible that the pendulum will swing back toward a greater acceptance of harsher physical punishment. A more optimal situation would be the development of more effective, nonphysical means of behavior control.

Looking back on my own life, I only remember experiencing one spanking with a hair brush. This occurred when I was around 2 years old and decided to use my mother's makeup to make myself beautiful. While she was in the bathroom I put on lipstick, rouge, and whatever else was handy, on my face. When she saw this, she became furious, turned me over her knee and spanked my derrière with a hairbrush. I was shocked and devastated. (I learned never to touch her makeup again.) I remember being shocked at the violence. Looking back on this, I don't think I needed the spanking, because I don't remember if she had told me her makeup was off limits. She never spanked me again. I always felt loved and never believed this affected me in a major negative way.

When looking at my behavior with my children, I realize that I was not a perfect mother. I did correct my son on occasion when he was young by slapping his hand and saying "No!" and as he grew older, I gave him a few slaps on his backside. He was an extremely active child who was always exploring. He walked at 10 months of age and climbed out of his crib at 11 months. He was very intelligent and highly mechanical. At age one, he weighed 35 lb. One night he climbed out of his crib when my husband and I were asleep, wandered around the house and plugged an iron into the wall and left it on, after which he went back to his room and climbed back into his crib. When I woke up, I smelled something burning and discovered that the carpet in the living room was on fire. Fortunately, we easily put it out, but pondered what to do about his wanderings. He was incapable of understanding the dangers of the world, but could access them easily.

His terrible 2's were terrible for me too! He explored everything and was fearless. He never walked, he ran. One afternoon when I thought he was asleep and taking a nap, I walked outside to pick up the newspaper. I happened to glance up at his upstairs window and saw him standing on his dresser, in front of the open window looking at me. I rushed into the house, ran into his room and snatched him off the high dresser just in time. (He had removed the drawers of the dresser, made stairs of them and ascended to the top.) He was one and a half at that time. I was desperate to protect his safety. I prayed he would survive childhood and sometimes had bad dreams of his getting hurt or killed. He did not seem to respond to anything but consistency, boundaries, and an occasional slap on the hand.

I sometimes wondered if I had been too strict. I thought since I was a "perfect" mother at that time, I believed everything would be easy and comfortable when I had children. I imagined I could explain things to any child and they would listen, respect my authority, and with occasional punishment they would become "perfect children". So, I did spank my son as well as use time outs, etc. At that time I was able to be a full time mother. (It was before I became a psychologist.) He did survive childhood and is a wonderful human being with the same drive and fearlessness he had as a child.

In retrospect, with all I know now, I believe corporeal punishment should be avoided if possible. There are so many other ways to consistently discipline that are effective. Accountability for one's actions must be taught to our children, so they can function in the world. Since every child is different, punishment must not only "fit the crime", but "fit the child."

My other children, two daughters, were very sensitive to any type of correction and did not need to be physically reprimanded. They went through the terrible 2's with very little upset compared to my son. I believe they would have been damaged by corporeal punishment in their early years. (One thing I learned from my personal experience is that every child is different from every other child.)

Many of you who are reading this may be wondering if you have made a mistake by either disciplining or not disciplining your children and how you have done this. You may wonder if you were "good enough" as I did. Remember, the most important thing is that your child felt your love and that it is impossible for any human being to be perfect all the time. The decision of whether to spank your child or not sometimes causes feelings of guilt in good enough mothers. Remember, you may spank or not spank and still be good enough.

# Emotional Abuse

The consequences of severe Physical Abuse are both emotional and Physical. The shock of physical trauma caused by a parent may cause emotional problems. The physical injuries may cause fractures, burns, scars, cuts, bruises, head injuries, brain damage, and even death. The emotional trauma of such abuse can cause intellectual and academic problems such as poor work in school as well as behavior problems. Victims of physical abuse may think differently than do non abused children. They may assume that others have hostile intentions. For example, if they were accidentally bumped by another child on the playground, they could assume that it was done on purpose. Their tendency is to attribute hostile intent to others.

They may also tend to have difficulties with interpersonal relationships. These victims have difficulties in forming strong interpersonal relationships because they are often insecurely attached to their parents and are frequently categorized as having a resistant or avoidant attachment to their caregivers. They may have trouble making friends because they have not developed the appropriate social skills.

Aggression is one of the most extensively documented effects of physical abuse. In a physically abusive household, aggression is modeled as a way to solve problems and as an appropriate behavior. Essentially, the children have been taught by their parents to behave this way. In addition, evidence from animal studies shows us that there may be a relationship between the experience of pain and aggression in children. There is a link between severe physical abuses in childhood to violent behavior in adulthood.

Physical abuse in childhood has also been liked with later substance abuse.

This includes alcohol as well as illegal drugs. This may be the result of the child's need to deaden the internal pain he or she feels as the result of the abuse.

Child victims of physical abuse generally have lower self-esteem than do their non-abused peers. They may suffer from depression and feelings of hopelessness. It has also been found that these children are more likely to have suicidal ideation.

Being physically abused as a child also increases the likelihood that the individual may develop Posttraumatic Stress Disorder (PTSD). (You may be familiar with PTSD as the illness war veterans sometime experience after an intense battle during which they felt threatened by death or serious injury or saw others experiencing this. The response of the soldier may have been to feel intense fear, helplessness or horror.) A person suffering from PTSD may re-experience the event, avoid reminders of the event, and show increased forms of arousal. Not only can physical abuse lead to post-traumatic stress disorder in some children, but in others, makes them more vulnerable to future violence.

Another category of abuse is labeled as Psychological Maltreatment. In psychological abuse, parents actively engage in behaviors that actively harm a child's mental health. An example would be a mother who yells at her child, calling him "stupid, lazy and no good", or a parent who threatens the life of a child by saying something like "I brought you into this world, and I darn well can take you out of it." Or "If you want to live to see your next birthday, you'll do what I say". When is this really damaging to a child? Damage occurs when he or she really believes it. Factors that determine this are age of the child, relationship history between mother and child, and how often it occurs. We know that how a mother views a child causes them to view themselves in the same way and often behave in that way. If they feel "stupid" for example, they may act "stupid" in school and may not work up to their potential. That said, good enough mothers may have found themselves saying such things on rare occasions when under extreme stress, and not actively harm their child when he knows he is deeply loved and his mother doesn't mean it.

Spurning is a word that comes to mind when we think of psychological abuse. This is parental behavior that is hostile toward and rejecting of the child. It includes belittling, degrading, shaming, ridiculing, publicly humiliating and repeatedly singling out one child for punishment or failing to reward one child. Good enough mothers do not do this.

Severe emotional abuse can create various emotional problems such as Borderline Personality Disorder, Social and Antisocial Functioning problems such as aggression, violence and delinquency, Learning problems, and even poor physical health.

# Sexual Abuse

Sexual Abuse may be defined as any sexual behavior directed toward a child by a person who has power over that child. Such behavior always involves a betrayal of the child's trust. Sexual abuse may occur with touch or not involve physical touch. Those involving touch may include masturbation, intercourse, fondling, oral sex, and anal or vaginal penetration with objects. Other types of sexual abuse that do not include physical touch may include, exhibitionism, leering and sexual suggestiveness or forcing a child to view a sexual act of any kind. Perpetrators of sexual abuse need not be strangers and may more likely be anyone in a position of power or trust such as fathers, uncles, cousins, stepfathers, siblings, mothers, teachers, babysitters, neighbors, grandparents, peers, clergy or even doctors.

Child sexual abuse can occur at any age, from infancy until the age of consent. It has been estimated that 20-40 percent of girls and 2-9 percent of boys are sexually abused by the time they reach age 18. Good enough mothers do not become sexually involved with their children or allow anyone else to do so. They protect them. However, it is depressing to note that sexual abuse can happen to our children at church, at camp, at school, or perhaps even in the bathroom of a movie theater. It happens to both boys and girls. Mothers are not always able to protect their children from sexual abuse.

The effects of sexual abuse extend far beyond childhood. Children who have been sexually abused have been robbed of their childhoods and have a loss of trust in others. They may have feelings of guilt and exhibit self-abusive behavior. Other consequences of sexual abuse are antisocial behavior, depression, identity confusion, loss of self-esteem, dissociative disorders, problems with intimacy later in life, self-destructive thinking and behavior, anxiety, Posttraumatic Stress Disorder, substance abuse, various personality disorders, eating disorders, disordered thinking, problems with social functioning, sexualized behavior, Dissociative Disorders, and Dissociated Memory.

Remember the case of Harry? He was abused as an altar boy by a Catholic priest. He experienced anxiety, suicidal ideation, guilt, self-abusive behavior, loss of self-esteem, problems with intimacy, Posttraumatic stress disorder, and substance abuse. His parents had no knowledge of what had happened. They were excellent parents and devastated when they found out what had happened to their son. This was an example of a danger in the world that had nothing to do with parenting. Even though he had a good enough mother, in the end, Harry killed himself with a drug overdose.

## Dissociative Disorders

To dissociate, means to cut off one part of oneself from another part of one's self. (Harry did not do this.) You may wonder how this could happen.

Extreme trauma that creates fear and pain can cause a child to block out the experience. Some children can actually put themselves into a hypnotic state where they feel no pain and don't even remember the experience. The question becomes, "What happens to the memory?"

The memory gets stored somewhere in the mind and may return to consciousness later. An event could occur many years later that reminds the person of what happened when they were a child going through the abuse. An example would be meeting someone that reminded them of the abuser. The meeting could trigger remembering. The memory would have become a dissociated memory during the time it was forgotten.

Sexual abuse and/or severe physical abuse that continues over time can cause a major dissociative disorder such as Dissociative Identity Disorder. The child becomes more and more skilled at dissociating the traumatic experiences and begins to compartmentalize or walls off parts of herself to deal with the pain and suffering. This compartmentalization can become so extreme; the compartments actually take on different names and ages. (This condition was called Multiple Personality Disorder in the past and is now called Dissociative Identity Disorder.)

The ability to dissociate is a healthy way to deal with inescapable trauma. Forgetting it happened could enable a child to go to school the next day and continue to learn, to socialize, make friends and grow up appearing normal.

The negative aspects of this solution are numerous. The child could have trouble remembering many things in his or her life because different parts of her might be present at different times and she would have blocked out her experiences. He or she may continue to use this process to avoid anything uncomfortable, that they may want to block out.

You may recall the case of Ellen whom I talked about briefly in the Chapter on memory. She forgot her whole therapy session when she cried and cried and was startled to have tears on her face and Kleenex in her lap.

The problem that brought her to therapy was depression. This case occurred in 1981, years before many therapists know how to recognize and treat dissociation. As you may remember, I did not know how to help Ellen until I went to the first meeting of the Society for the Study of Multiple Personality and Dissociative Disorders. I arranged consultation time with experts on dissociation who advised me to help Ellen relax in the next session and ask if there were other parts of her who could help me understand what had happened. (Fortunately I had been fully trained in hypnosis and had been teaching it to Medical students so I could understand the power of the mind to affect the body.)

As I helped Ellen relax, I was somewhat startled when Ellen's face seemed to change slightly, her voice lowered, and she said, "We have been watching you for a year and we know you are trying to help Ellen. We trusted you enough to let you know we are here." I asked how many parts of Ellen were there. She said, "My name is Sue and there are three of us here. There are more in other places". I thanked her for the information and told "Sue" they could return to where they had been. I was somewhat relieved when the Ellen I knew returned when requested. Ellen looked around the room and asked, "What happened?" She stated that she did not remember anything since she had begun to relax.

I decided to refer Ellen to someone else who had more expertise in working with dissociation. I explained what little I knew about dissociation to Ellen and told her about everything that had transpired during our session. She shared with me things she had never told anyone. Some of her revelations included the description of major memory lapses, finding things among her belongings she did not remember buying, sometimes feeling that she was outside her body watching herself, finding herself in clothes she did not remember putting on, believing that she had not eaten or had anything to drink for days, yet feeling full and being in perfect health, and often being mistaken for someone else. She was also often accused of doing things she did not remember doing and when she denied that she had done them, was accused of lying. She was very emotional and cried when she agreed that she needed help.

The following week I searched for either a psychiatrist or psychologist who had experience treating dissociation. I could find no one in Milwaukee, only in Chicago. One of the experts there agreed to take her as a patient. When Ellen came in for her weekly visit, I told her about my findings. She became distraught and said she could not travel to Chicago every week, nor could she afford the cost as she was working in order to complete her college training.

One of the turning points in my career was when I decided to see her as a patient for a nominal fee and have regular consultations with one of the top experts in Chicago so I could learn how best to treat her. Ellen and I discussed the situation and considered all the pros and cons. She knew I would be learning as we worked together.

As we worked together, I learned how to access the different parts of Ellen's mind, develop a relationship with them and then help Ellen know them and slowly access their memories and experiences as she could handle the information.

Several of the parts of Ellen reported traumatic sexual abuse by her father over a long period of time. Other parts of Ellen reported some physical abuse by her father. (Ellen's father had passed away several years before her therapy started.)

As we worked, I discovered that the compartmentalized memories were complete. For example, Sue was able to share a complete memory, but did not have any feelings about it. Another part of Ellen who called herself Sandy, cried a lot as she shared the feelings of the abuse. Still another aspect of Ellen was very angry about what her father had done and threw things. She learned to vent her anger on a punching bag.

Ellen was extremely intelligent and was able to continue attending school as well as working at her job as a secretary throughout her therapy. Therapy was intense. Ellen began to remember all of the things that had happened to her in childhood as she learned to communicate with the parts of herself that had this knowledge. (Many of her memories were corroborated by her sister.) As we worked, she had fewer and fewer dissociative symptoms. Ellen reached a point where she knew all the parts of herself and no longer had amnesia or "lost time". Then a very interesting thing occurred. Ellen graduated from college with a Bachelor's Degree and she realized that she had always wanted to attend Law School. This required completion of an entrance examination, the

LSAT (The Law School Aptitude Test). What happened over the next year seemed somewhat surreal. Ellen studied for the test and took it. Unfortunately she did not have a high enough score to meet the entrance requirements. She was very upset and told me that the reason she did not do well was because all the different parts of her were arguing about which was the right answer. (She had scored in the 75th percentile.)

Ellen decided to take the test a second time. She not only studied for the test again, but asked all the different parts of her to let her do it alone and not distract her. "They" all agreed. They did not interrupt her. Ellen still did not meet the entrance requirements. (She had scored in the 85th percentile.) In therapy we worked together to analyze what had occurred that might have prevented her from doing better. She determined that she might do better if somehow she could access information from all the parts of her. Ellen developed a plan.

Her Plan was that she would take the test one more time. This time all her "parts" would work together. Ellen would first answer all the questions she was sure of. Then, another part would come forward and answer all they knew, followed by several "others", taking turns, until the test was completed. This time Ellen passed with flying colors. She came out in the 99th percentile and was accepted into Law School.

Ellen's tenacity enabled her to not only finish law school, but to realize the importance of integrating all parts of herself to function normally. Her therapy took about 5 years. Ellen married a lawyer she had met during law school. She later became a successful attorney and became a good enough mother of 2 children who are doing well. Ellen has a normal life and is no longer depressed or dissociative.

As mentioned in the chapter on memories, the diagnosis of Dissociative Identity Disorder and repressed or dissociated memory came into question during the late 1990's. It had become a popular diagnosis of the 80's and had previously been labeled Multiple Personality Disorder. Perhaps some well-meaning therapists misdiagnosed it or suggested abuse that never occurred.

It is important for all mothers and fathers to be aware of the effects of abuse. Good enough mothers need to know about all the pitfalls that can occur to harm their child and do their best to protect them. Ellen's mother did not know what her husband had done to Ellen. She worked as a secretary for a law firm outside the home to support the family, knew her husband had emotional problems, but did not believe he would be a danger to Ellen if she left them alone together. She was a good enough mother who I hope has taken herself off the hot seat for being unaware what Ellen had experienced and now knowing she had been unable to protect her.

One thing I learned about Ellen's mother is how much she loved Ellen and how much Ellen loved her. I believe that love may be what helped Ellen pursue her dreams and complete her therapy.

As I thought of all the types of abuse and how good enough mothers do not abuse their children even though they are not perfect, I considered the other factors present in the world today that can affect children in a negative way and may be dangerous to their physical and mental health. The effects of the recent technological revolution and social change within the last 30 years presents challenges to families never experienced previously. Parents are now called upon to deal with these challenges!

# Chapter 6

# THE TECHNOLOGICAL REVOLUTION

*I fly away to a faraway land*
*A land free of pain*
*A land of my choice and wildest imaginings*
*To be who I want*
*To get what I want*
*To find love and excitement and freedom*
*A land to learn ways to control*
*It is the reality I want!*
*Is it real?*

The technological revolution has been exponentially gaining momentum for the last thirty years at an amazing speed! Many parents, psychologists, psychiatrists, pediatricians, and clergy share concern about the effects of these developments upon children as well as adults. They are having a profound effect upon the relationships between mothers and their children.

The development of technology has been implicated as a factor to account for some of the negative behaviors in children and young adults that we are seeing more of as time goes by. These include school shootings, drugs, sexual acting out, and violence of all kinds. They can be related to social, environmental, and technological influences. Television, texting, and the internet usage influences child behavior and development to a major degree. It is important for mothers to be aware of the dangers they may pose to children as they develop.

As I use and enjoy all the technological tools we have today, I have been experiencing a sense of growing unease over the last 10 years as I realize the impact their influence could have upon children and some adults who are malleable and perhaps unable to discern whether something is real or unreal.

I lived in Waukesha, Wisconsin for one year in the 1980's and remember it as a quiet upper-middle class community of friendly welcoming people. About a month ago I got word of the terrible tragedy that recently occurred there. The question was: "What inspired two preteen girls to attempt murder?"

Two 12 year old girls tried to murder another 12 year old girl. According to a local newspaper "They were charged with attempted first-degree intentional homicide for allegedly stabbing their young classmate 19 times and each face up to 65 years in prison. According to police, the girls planned the crime for months in advance. They invited the victim to a sleep over at one of their homes on Friday, originally plotting to cover the victim's mouth with duct tape and then stab her in the neck, before running away. Instead, they decided that they would lure the victim to a nearby park the next day. One girl told police that she knew that the park bathroom had a drain in the floor where the blood could go down.

The girls told their victim that they were going to the park to go bird-watching and play hide-and-seek. They passed by a public bathroom and some trees and then began to stab her."

Fortunately, a bicyclist saw the child as she crawled out of the woods and got help for her in time. At this time she seems to be recuperating well.

The motivation for this event appeared to be the internet. Newspaper accounts stated, "The two young suspects were apparently fascinated with the horror stories on the website Creepypasta Wiki. They believed that the internet-born legend of Slenderman was real. The girls told police that they had to kill their friend to prove their loyalty to him. Both girls had actually planned to hike into the northern Wisconsin Nicolet National Forest after the murder to join Slenderman, who they believed lived in a mansion there."

It was reported in one newspaper that one of the girl's parents were also fascinated with Slenderman and seemed drawn to the macabre. There is an unmistakable sense that the girls lost touch with reality and were influenced by the internet. It is impossible for every parent to monitor everything their child sees on the internet, but parents can also lose sight of what is damaging to their child. Good enough mothers need to become aware of and know how to protect their children from these dangers. The statistics and descriptions that follow are paraphrased from the book, "Closer Together, Further Apart" (2012) by Robert Weiss and Jennifer Schneider. I interspersed my interpretations with some of their Information.

## Overview

Technology has changed our world. It is important to understand and have gratitude for its benefits, which are huge. Digital technology has brought amazing interconnectivity with relationships. One can communicate with others for the other side of the world. (There are over 2 billion internet users worldwide, that is nearly 1/3 of the planet.)

Technology (which includes cell phones, cable television, and the internet) can help families stay connected. It can be used for information gathering and processing, can stimulate political and social activism, provide help in diagnosing and managing illness, communicating with friends and family, developing new relationships, and can be used for entertainment. The development of Wikipedia, (which is a free international online encyclopedia) is the single most commonly used general reference site in the world. There is a website to help parents find nonviolent video games for children. (It is commonsensemedia.org.)

People born after 1980 never knew the world without these technological advances.) A survey in 2009 indicated that one half of all teens in the U.S. logged on to a social media website more than once a day, and more than one fourth of the teens more than 10 times a day. More than three quarters of the teens owned cell phones and 88% texted regularly. I believe these statistics are much higher today in 2014. Technology is here to stay. All parents are faced with decisions about how to handle issues related to technological growth. It is both a blessing and a danger.

Recent statistics indicate that 97% of teenagers under 18 spend an average of 13 hours per week playing video games. The typical child will have spent 10,000 hours gaming by age 21. (This does not include time spent using other technology.) Seventy one to seventy six percent of their day is now spent engaged in digital technology. We do not yet know about the major long term effects of this engagement. I am amazed at this magnitude of this involvement!

It is clearly important for children to learn how to use modern technology. Young people today are learning both in and out of school, differently from the way their parents did. These differences originate from their immersion in digital technology. There are estimates that by the time they are in their 20's, they will have spent more than 30,000 hours on the internet and playing video games. These hours will be spent at a time when their brains are particularly sensitive to outside influences. There is recent research that demonstrates that that violent videogames can actually change mental reflexes and habits as well as the way young people learn and absorb information.

Children born after 1980 don't necessarily read from left to right, or from beginning to end. They are more sensitive to visual icons than older people, and absorb more information when it is presented with visual images. Many do not like to read books and can get information by going to Google.

It is important for good enough mothers to understand what the influences are outside of themselves, schools, and families that they must deal with in order to remain a good enough parent. The following dangers are present in the cyber world of today.

# Cyber bullying

It is important to look at both the pros and cons when dealing with technology. Cyber bullying has been identified as an occurrence that has been harmful to children. It is defined as the deliberate, repeated, and hostile use of the internet and related technologies to harm other people and is primarily perpetrated by and against children.

In 2010 a fifteen year old Massachusetts girl, hanged herself after being bullied and humiliated via text messages and on Face-book. The bullying had gone on for nearly three months by multiple students at her high school.

That same year a student at Rutgers University set up a hidden webcam in his dorm room to spy on his eighteen year old roommate. Unexpectedly, he captured his roommate engaged in a consensual sexual encounter with another man. He sent out texts and tweets encouraging others to view the recorded encounter online. Three days later the roommate jumped to his death from the George Washington Bridge in New York City.

## Sexting

Since the advent of computers and smart phones with built in digital cameras and webcams, it is easy for anyone to take a provocative snapshot of themselves and send it to another person. The recipient may then choose to send it to another person or post it online for public viewing.

Boyfriends or girlfriends break up they have been known to "punish" each other by posting the pictures online.

This is also considered illegal and pornographic. Participants have been arrested and charged.

## Online Porn

In this digital age, endless amounts of soft and hardcore porn are available for anyone who goes looking for it and also for people who aren't looking for it. All a child needs to do is find a porn site, click a button that says they are 18 and access is granted. Children's exposure to adult pornography is extremely common. A 2008 survey of 594 university students revealed that 93% of male students and 62% of female students reported having seen hardcore online pornography prior to age 18. Anticipating and coping with a child's unintentional exposure to porn should now be a part of every good enough parent's responsibility. Parents today must educate their children about healthy intimate sexuality or their child's sexual education will occur prematurely by internet porn.

## Online Predators

A serious risk to children is possible exposure to sexual predators through social media and other online connections. In 2000, Kathrin Tarbox wrote a blog describing her experience as a young teen who barely escaped being raped after making such a connection. Tarbox had connected with another child in a young people's chat room and eventually agreed to meet her suitor in person. That "boy" turned out to be an adult predator. Her family, searching for her by checking her phone and computer, located her in this man's hotel room in time. They rescued her moments before she was to be physically assaulted. There are many friend finder websites where online predators are searching for vulnerable child-victims.

## Online Gaming

Much has been written about online gaming. My first experience with the risks involved was in the mid 80's. My husband and I often socialized with a couple who lived nearby.

Scott and Elise had three children, two girls and a boy. The boy, Andrew, was 14 and the girls, Debbie age 10 and Anne age 7. Scott and Elise both worked to support the family and were very proud of their children. They seemed to be excellent parents who loved their children dearly and worked hard to provide everything the children needed. The children were involved in various activities and sports. They had a computer that their son loved to use. All the children did well in school, had friends and seemed well adjusted. I believe Scott and Elise were good parents.

I remember the evening early in January when Elise called sobbing to tell us that Andrew had killed himself. She asked us to come and be with them until more family could arrive. (Andrew had hung himself in his bedroom by standing on a chair with a noose around his neck and jumping off.) By the time we got there the body had already been removed. Scott and Elise were in shock. They had no idea why he would do this terrible thing. We sat with them for hours as they dealt with their pain, confusion, and anger. The little girls were also shocked. (It was Debbie who had found the body.) No one had sensed or knew of any depression or problems that Andrew could have had. While we were there, the family called Andrew's friends and asked if they knew of any possible reason for Andrew's suicide. They finally spoke to one friend who told Scott that Andrew had been obsessed with the internet game, Dungeons and Dragons. He mentioned that Andrew believed that he could "leave this world and return to it" as in the reality of the game. Andrew had left no suicide note.

Before this happened I had never heard of Dungeons and Dragons.

After this painful incident, I began to explore what had happened to other young people as a result of this type of online gaming. (There were at least 20 cases of suicide or murder that I read about that implicated Dungeons and Dragons as a cause.) I decided to go on line and visited several game sites as well as played some of the games that have been implicated in school shootings and violence to experience for myself what I thought about them as a causal agent of violence in young people.

I visited the web sites for "Call of Duty", "Grand Theft Auto", "Dungeons and Dragons", and "Slender Man". They were all based on games of violence and killing.

As I played the games, I felt like I was the character in the action. The character I created to represent me could do un-imaginable things. I found myself in situations where I was felt forced to kill others in order to survive within the game. I could act out any fantasy I pleased and survive. I could also interact with other characters that were fantasy representations of other players. There was violence and murder everywhere. I realized how addictive these games could be. My adrenalin was certainly rising. I forced myself to continue to better understand the impact of the games. As I did so I became extremely alarmed about how these games affect both children and adults. Common sense, apart from research, tells anyone that the games teach violence and lack of empathy to whoever watches them. When children experience virtual reality they are being taught that is the way of the world.

After I actually experienced the games I better understood how they attract both children and adults. The website asked how old I was in order to access the games. I could have told them I was any age I wanted to be. Anyone who could navigate the website could play the game. I discovered that if I really wanted to become an expert game player, I could invest in an XBOX1, which "brings together the best exclusive games, the most advanced multiplayer and entertainment experiences you won't find anywhere else..." (The cost is $399.00.)

# Violent On-Line Game Characteristics

Characteristics common to all were:

<u>The creation of an imaginary world</u> (the player experiences a virtual reality which produces feelings in the players of actually being there)

<u>Fear filled emotional scenes and threats to survival and Isolation</u> (by removing them from traditional support structures within the game. They have none of these supports within that reality and "anything goes".)

<u>Physical torture and killings</u> (focus was upon killings and torture for the acquisition of wealth and survival. I had the power to do anything and was forced into the experience of killing others in order to play the game.)

<u>Control</u> (demand upon players for all encompassing and total loyalty, control and allegiance to a leader.)

<u>Situational Ethics</u> (any act in the game can be justified in the mind of the player; there is no morality, good seldom triumphs.)

<u>Traditional values and belief systems restructured</u> (players align themselves with special deities or leaders they select. Patron deities suggested and occult gods are included.)

<u>Loss of self-control</u> (Loss of self-control is experienced within the game. There is little choice.)

<u>Degradation</u> (Pain and torture are heavily involved in sadistic, sexual situations with pornographic and sexual themes which included defilement of innocence.) Some of you may be familiar with the case of Adam Lanza, the 20 year old man who was behind the horrific shooting rampage in Newtown, Connecticut. It has been learned that he had been obsessed with the online game, "Call to Duty". Police found thousands of dollars' worth of graphically violent video games in the home Lanza shared with his mother. Detectives working the scene are exploring whether Adam Lanza might have been emulating the shooting range of a video-game scenario as he moved from room to room in Sandy Hook school.

## Television

I have noticed over the last few years that television has an increased level of violent content as well as sexually explicit material. It has been estimated that 60% of all programming has violent content. Vampire shows are currently very popular. The average child in the United States spends about 25 hours a week in front of the television. The American Academy of Pediatrics issued a recommendation that children watch no more than one to two hours of "quality" television a day. Children under age 2 should not watch television at all, and older kids should not have televisions in their bedrooms. A few programs teach children important skills such as reading, math, science or problem solving. These can help children learn. Non educational shows have been linked with poorer school performance. Violent programming has been linked with violent or antisocial behavior in children, depending on the degree of violence and the total number of violent programs the child watches.

I was having lunch one day in a local restaurant and noticed a party of about 12 people seated very close to me. There were 3 children in the group who appeared to be around 1 year old. The adults present were both men and women who were very busy socializing. There appeared to be a lot of affection in the group and all were in a good mood. I noticed that there was a little boy seated in a high chair with his back to me. He appeared to be about 10 months old and was very quiet. I realized he was staring at a TV set which was propped up on the table in front of his high chair. I decided to discover what was so absorbing to him and watched the TV over his shoulder from about 5 feet away.

The program he was watching was animated and included various cartoon characters who were hitting each other and pushing each other as well as running around, chasing, and hiding from each other. There were buildings and streets.

As I mentioned earlier, the American Academy of Pediatricians recommends that children under 2 years of age should not watch TV at all. The child's parents appeared to be using TV as a baby sitter.

One of the major activities on TV is the commercials. Advertising, being visual, is very compelling. A large percentage of time is spent trying to get viewers to buy drugs, food, toys, and various gimmicks. These commercials are teaching both children and adults to desire "things" to make them happy. From a psychological perspective I can appreciate the creative and innovative methods they use. Many of the commercials are hypnotic. All of us are being influenced to become "better consumers".

An added negative effect of heavy TV watching is obesity. Children do not get enough exercise if they are watching TV for long hours as well as consuming large amounts of high calorie food possibly advertised in one of the commercials.

## Cell Phones

Twenty two percent of children, ages 6 to 9 own a cell phone, with the average percentage climbing to 84 percent by the time they are in their teens. Widespread cell phone use has revolutionized the culture of the modern child.

Positive aspects of cell phone use are the facilitation of communication with their friends and family as well as parents being more connected to their child wherever they are.

Negative outcomes can be considered a form of "addiction". Some children feel they "must" continue texting in order to keep up with friends. They may also become addicted to various internet "hazards" discussed previously such as sexting, pornography, internet predators, and violent online gaming. Addiction is an uncontrollable compulsion to do something that may be detrimental to one's life or is inappropriate at that time.

Excessive time spent on cell phones may indicate depression and anxiety in children. Heavy child cell phone users also rated lower in their ability to express their emotions.

There is a continued debate about whether or not the radiation from cell phones causes cancer in children and adults. The jury is still out on that issue.

As I was pursuing the question of "What causes criminality and violence in people?" I was thinking about what good enough mothers can do to deal with the negative influences of our advanced technology.

## Recommendations

Children who carry histories of child abuse and neglect are at risk from early exposure to pornography, excessive online gaming and reduced "live social engagement." Being exposed to the dangerous online world poses great risk of harm.

Exposure to violence affects children as well as adults. It elicits violent behavior and deadens empathy and compassion. Children who are exposed to violence whether actual and in the home, or in the virtual world are being taught to be violent and lack the ability to use the critical thinking that most adults can use to know that violence is undesirable. Most adults can realize the unreality and undesirability of the values in that virtual world. I wondered why it is difficult to find video games that teach love, compassion, tolerance and the joy of helping others.

I have been focusing on how to be a good enough mother, so almost all mothers can be taken off the hot seat for problems caused by technology that parents are unable to control. It is important to know what has been recommended by pediatricians as well as determining how to protect your child in the best way possible. It is a growing challenge today for good enough mothers to decide what is "good enough" mothering when dealing with technology.

The things parents are doing to protect their children from the dangers of the digital revolution that were recommended by The American Academy of Pediatrics are:

1) Discouraging screen media exposure for children less than two years of age.
2) Limiting the total of entertainment screen time to less than 1 to 2 hours a day.
3) Keeping TV and Internet-connected devices out of the child's bedroom.
4) Monitoring what media children are using and accessing.
5) Co-viewing TV, movies, and videos with children and teenagers, and using this as a way of discussing important family issues.
6) Modeling active parenting by establishing a family home use plan for all media.
7) Establishing reasonable, but firm rules about cell phones, texting, Internet and social media use.

Other things some parents are doing are to disallow cell phones that have internet access, keeping the computer in a central location, and being vigilant as to the content of what their children are experiencing on line.

I met with a group of mothers who were so concerned about the digital revolution, they were home schooling their children as well as following the guidelines above.

It is important to provide exciting "here and now" activities. One of the most negative aspects of the digital revolution is the time spent out of the "here and now". This limits time for learning to interact with others in traditional ways.

Awareness of one's surroundings, learning to communicate face to face, experiencing the importance of the real world, learning how to experience the nuances within individual people, animals, plants, insects, and groups is priceless. When I take a walk early every morning, I can enjoy the rabbit running across my path, perhaps pause to examine an ant hill, smell the dew on the flowers, hear the breeze rustling the tree leaves, and note the red blooms on a huge cactus at the bottom of my driveway. If I were texting, listening to music, or talking on my cell phone, I would have missed my entire walk.

Walks may not be interesting to everyone, but many here and now activities are; such as experiencing participation in sports, picnics, travel, etc. A good enough mother protects her child from danger. Some of the aspects of the digital revolution are extremely dangerous. All mothers can do is their best as we find ways to protect their children. Since we are not perfect or able to control everything, we can hope and prod society to accept the present negative aspects of digital technology as it relates to children and do something to change it. The following tongue in cheek "recipe" is very thought provoking:

## How to Dehumanize a Child

The first thing to do is to take one healthy normal baby and put him in front of the TV as soon as his eyes focus. (There are numerous programs to capture his attention.) You can put him there anytime you are busy or if he is restless. Put a TV in his room. As soon as he is able, teach him how to text and buy him a cell phone. If you can afford it, also buy him a computer and show him how to use it. Place it in his room. Play violent video games with him. If he misbehaves, send him to his room. Text constantly. Always watch TV during mealtime. Communicate with him by texting whenever possible. Buy food and toys for him that he sees advertised on TV. Keep yourself busy on the internet. Never read to him, don't let any of his friends into the house. Buy him a smart phone as soon as possible. (Let it babysit him.) Avoid talking with him. Eliminate family outings such as picnics or games. Leave him home alone for long periods. Don't worry about who his friends are. Let him be. Most importantly, never tell him you love him.

Unfortunately, the above instructions are sometimes carried out in some homes today. Thirty nine women in my pilot study said they were also very concerned about the effects of the media and struggled to protect their children from possible negative influences. The remaining 8 women I polled were mildly concerned.

I have written in detail dangers of the technological revolution that can cause major problems for children, as well as damage relationships between parent and child. It is also important to consider what rapid social changes are occurring that impact children and mothers of today.

# Chapter 7

# SOCIAL CHANGE

*Mother Knows Best*

*Now you know and then you don't*
*Safe and serene, but then the leap*
*Gone from sight the known way*
*Like a ship that drifted out in the bay*
*What is best and what is good*
*To help you grow the best you could*
*I need to learn all over again*
*How to help and how to know*
*My ways as mother, to teach you love*

The world has changed dramatically in the last 50 years! As I focus on mothering. I am amazed at how mothers are called upon to deal with so many more things than they did 50 years ago.

Social change has had a huge impact on mothers, mothering, and mother-child relationships. My considerations of these changes took me out of my fairy tale completely. I realized that I had experienced being a single parent for only a short period of time, but had all the advantages of a great education and a supportive mother who enjoyed babysitting. I felt a little guilty as I realized the impact of change upon mothers today in comparison to what I had experienced.

## Future Shock

Alvin Toffler in his seminal book, "Future Shock", published in the 1970's, helped prepare us for this escalation of progress. He wrote about the repercussions of technological growth, but did not address the effects of technological growth specifically upon relationships between mothers and children. The speedy technological revolution has caused a generation gap between the children who were born into it and their parents who were not. It is sometimes difficult for one generation to understand the other as they are accustomed to communicating differently.

When I questioned mothers in my pilot study about their stresses as mothers today, I realized that I had been somewhat insulated from reality. Many of the mothers I spoke with were single mothers, trying to be good enough mothers alone. Many of them had little support from other family members or society. All the mothers of children who still lived at home reported stress on relationships, guilt at not having enough time with their children, little time to relax, almost no time for themselves, and exhaustion. This was sobering. I remembered the stresses I had experienced raising my 3 children with a lot of help and had difficulty comprehending how mothers today can function so well and survive emotionally and physically. I discovered the book by Katrina Alcorn, "Maxed Out, American Moms on the Brink" (2013). Alcorn's book provided the following statistics and described her experiences and stresses as she raised her children in today's world. I paraphrased some of the following information from her book as well as added some of my own thoughts.

Parents are living longer today. This generation is the only one that has not had a higher standard of living than their parents. Most parents cannot depend upon their children to support them financially as they age. Many adult children are forced to depend upon their aging parents for subsistence, even though they are skilled workers. Resources are limited. This new situation affects relationships between adult children and their parents. Parents and children may grow to resent each other due to the unexpected stresses placed upon them. Adult children may have hoped for an inheritance and feel resentful or fearful as their parents continue to live and may marry again in old age. This may cause a threat to an expected inheritance. Aging parents may have had expectations of more support from their children than they are able to provide due to their busy schedules. Mother bashing and hurt feelings can occur as a result for both parents and children.

Today 70% of American children live in households where all adults are employed. I was surprised to discover that families today earn 29% less in buying power than they did thirty years earlier. Middle-income families earn 13% less. Only professional families are making more than they did in 1979. They are making 7% more, but work longer hours than ever before. The impact of these statistics is profound. Stresses on families and mothers in particular are extreme. Mothers and fathers are working longer hours for less and less money. This deprives children of much needed attention and the experiences of loving care.

It is evident that we lack the social and systemic supports that are needed in order to continue good enough parenting as well as share our talents with the world. Being stressed out to the extreme is making many mothers ill. In Japan the word Karoshi means "death by overwork". Americans are now working longer hours than the Japanese. Mothers in the U.S. are receiving less financial and social support than those of any developed country.

## Changing Roles

Almost everyone has been impacted by the recession of 2008. Job loss not only creates stress because of lack of money, but may create even deeper problems for children and parents because of role confusion. Families have been accustomed to stable roles as to who does what within the family. Who works? Who mothers? Who cleans? Who cooks? Who does outside work? Who repairs things? The questions go on and on. Some families are better able to make these adjustments than others.

One of the women in my pilot study was Sheila. She was the mother of 3 children in a Hispanic family. Sheila worked as a waitress and could always find work. Her husband, Jose, never learned to speak English and spoke only Spanish. He worked as a plumber for a construction company. Jose earned a good salary and often was able to work overtime. Sheila and Jose both worked hard and got along well. After the 2008 recession the housing industry crashed and the construction company went bankrupt. Jose could not find work even though he tried and tried. Sheila became the sole breadwinner.

Jose became depressed and did not want to spend time at home. He began to drink alcohol every day and went to a local casino to gamble. Jose was miserable and refused to help at home in any way. He withdrew emotionally from Sheila, the children and his relatives. Sheila became so ill from working extra shifts that she could not work at all. Jose would not help. He was not able to adjust to a new role within the marriage. Relatives of the family pitched in to help with child care as well as some money. The last I heard, nothing had improved for Jose. He is still unable to find work and seems to have given up on life.

The aforementioned case is an example of inability to change roles and role confusion. When socio-economic changes occur, the stresses they create may disrupt family member's roles. Repercussions can cause other family members to change roles. Teenagers could be asked to get a job in order help financially.

## Changes in What Women Want and What Women Do

In 2009 the American birthrate slid to 2.0. In 2011, it slid to 1.9, the lowest rate ever recorded. For the first time, Americans are having fewer babies than the French or English. Many women say they have decided not to have children because they realize they would be asking too much of themselves to do so.

These developments are a concern of not only psychologists, but sociologists, anthropologists, and perhaps some politicians. I asked myself who will be raising our future generations? Will they be able to do it without using technology as a baby sitter? Our wonderful technology with the dark side of potentially dehumanizing a child could create serious societal problems. In 1964 most mothers considered themselves "Homemakers". They did not work outside the home and were quintessential mothers. Feminism had just begun. Mothers cooked, cleaned, did the laundry, and focused on their children most of the time.

Women went to college, but few studied science, math, or business. Most of them who had completed a college education had gone to school to have something to "fall back on" in case they did not marry, or some tragedy happened that, god forbid, made it necessary for them to work. Also, college was a good place to meet "the man of their dreams". There was the un-verbalized hope that this would occur before they finished college. Most middle class women were married before or shortly after graduation. It was considered "improper" to have sex before marriage. Children who grew up at that time expected their mothers to be there for them at all times. Fathers were gone a lot and were the "breadwinners" of the family.

Rural families who farmed worked more as a team. However, mothers were the primary caregivers of their children, as well as part of the team to complete farming chores.

As time went by, social mores changed. Women were experiencing more equality and a higher percentage of them worked outside their homes. By the 1980's many of them were forced for economic reasons to have the opportunity to "individuate". Some of them began to find out who they were apart from their roles as "mother". Some found new interests and many developed new skills. They discovered opportunities to work up to their intellectual and emotional potentials and explored the world of work, education, and personal growth. The divorce rate began to grow. Divorces affected their styles of mothering as well, in some cases, traumatizing their children.

I was caught up in these societal changes also. It was during this time that I went back to school to earn a Master's and a Ph.D. degree in Psychology. I was concerned about the effects on my children as well as my spouse. I thought all was well as I had a fellowship that paid my tuition and gave a stipend that covered a cleaning lady. My children had already started school and my mother was home when the children arrived there after school. I believed it was an ideal situation. It wasn't until they grew up that they told me of their resentments.

As the speed of social change escalated, the number of single parent families grew. The "good enough mother" was becoming more and more stretched in many different directions and often felt conflicted. Being a good enough mother was hard to juggle with becoming a breadwinner, individuating, taking care of the home, as well as learning new things and keeping up with cultural change.

Today, there are many styles of good enough mothering. Some mothers are staying at home with their children again and may be home schooling them.

At the other extreme, good enough mothers may be involved with a high powered career and hire help to clean, cook, and take care of their children when they are not there.

Some good enough mothers are single women who work and may be struggling to keep food on the table. Still others may be gay and lesbian-parented families where "mothering" is shared.

As I had explored all the qualities necessary to be a good enough mother, I realized that the most important one is love. After I really believed that no one is perfect, I knew that I had finally forgiven myself as well as my own mother for not being perfect.

It is inevitable that all children have baggage, either from their parents, and others in their lives, or traumatic experiences. "Baggage" is defined as something in your past that affected you negatively or positively at the time it happened, but is still stored in your unconscious. If it was something negative like my mother being obsessed with money, anything that reminded me of money could elicit similar feelings to the ones I had when she kept telling me about money. This had actually occurred in my relationship with my husband.

Baggage from something positive might cause a person to have expectations of someone close to them that were inappropriate for the situation. For example, if when a husband was a child, his mother always baked regularly and had goodies waiting for him when he got home from school, his baggage might be the expectation that his wife bake regularly, even though she was unable to do so and working longer hours at her job than he was.

## Different Family Constellations

Again, the simplest definition of a "mother" is: the primary caregiver, who unconditionally loves their child, cares for him, protects him, disciplines him and teaches him to love. There is an aspect of connection and empathy that is different from that between other caregivers in the family constellation. It is possible to have more than one "mother" in the family constellation. It is evident that both biological father and mother in a two parent grouping can function as "mother". There seems to be a growing trend for this to happen as the pressures build for everyone to be able to do everything.

Physical touch in the form of comforting, caressing, and expressing love is critical. Research indicates the importance of this physical connection throughout the animal kingdom. "Mothering" can be done by either a man or woman.

After exploring the different types of families: Two parents (when one stays home and the other works to support the family), Single parent families, two parents (when both work), and gay and lesbian-parented families as well as mothering by extended family members, I found that they can all be effective. Research indicates that these many different types of families can raise healthy normal children. Both men and women can fulfill the role of mother. (Sometimes families have 2 mothers or more.) Traditionally, mothers were women and today most "mothers" are women.

I remember I was once asked by the court to complete custody evaluation of a couple who were divorcing. Bob and Ida had twins; Leslie and Sarah. The couple was fairly nontraditional as Ida was the breadwinner and Bob stayed home with the children. He had "mothered" them since they were 6 weeks old. Leslie and Sara were 8 years old at the time of my evaluation. They were well adjusted, normal healthy happy girls and did well in school. Bob appeared to be a kindly, affectionate man who was intelligent and well adjusted. When I observed him in my waiting room with the children, they appeared to be relaxed and sat close to him as he read to them. They appeared to be snuggling up to him and giggled at the story he was reading.

When I observed them with their mother, they behaved more formally and sat on the other side of the room. Bob had never had or wanted a job outside of the home and said he loved parenting the girls. He stated "It is my life!" He even baked cakes for the PTA.

I also interviewed the girls separately. Both volunteered that they loved both their parents, but they did not get to spend much time with their mother as she was "always at work" and usually worked late. When I asked them about what they did every day, they described going places with their Dad and mentioned that he had recently taught them how to bake a cake.

It was clear that Bob was performing the mother role in the household with the children. They felt nurtured and loved. Ida loved them too, but did not nurture them in the ways they needed at that time. The court awarded primary custody to Bob. Ida had to pay child support and saw them every other weekend. This happened in the late 1980's and was a first for that local court.

Ida was a business woman and CEO of a large corporation. She was also well adjusted and intelligent, although more reserved. Ida had desired primary custody of the girls because she thought they should be with their "mother". She had planned to hire a nanny to take care of them and drive them to various school and after-school functions.

The commonalities present in successful parenting in addition to the ones mentioned above were: 1) clarity of roles (Who can be depended upon to do what?), 2) predictability of parental behavior, 3) knowing they are loved, protected and wanted (Physical connection and nurturance are present from birth.), 4) understanding the rules and receiving discipline appropriate to age and situation and, 5) receiving adequate enrichment opportunities to further development.

The importance of physical touch in the form of cuddling with affection cannot be over emphasized. Since mothers, who are most often women, are responsible for "humanizing" their offspring. They must not only love them, but teach them about empathy, values, tolerance, and connection to others. They must also teach them how to control their aggression and any violent tendencies they may have. One of the ways they teach this is by modeling the desired behavior. This means they must be able to do this themselves, not just talk about it.

## Victims of Transition

I began to wonder if my daughter and I were victims of the transition of parenting functions. When I went to graduate school full time to work on my Doctorate, my son was in High School and very busy with all kinds of activities. He did not expect or want the kind of attention I had once given him. My youngest daughter was accustomed to my going to school part time as I had begun this process when she was two years old. My mother role for her included my career. My middle child had become accustomed to a more intense degree of my attention, absorption and time. When I didn't car pool her or take the time to buy her a new jacket, she felt abandoned and perhaps unloved. I, in turn, remember feeling worried and a little guilty about taking time away from my family to pursue my dream of a Doctorate, even though my own mother who was widowed at that time suggested that if I wanted to go to school, she would love to be there for my children when they got home from school or stay home with them if they were ill. My guilt may have been perceived by my daughter, causing her to feel even worse. It may also have changed my behavior toward her at that time.

Many mothers have made the transition from "stay at home mom" to career woman. Some children have been called upon to change their role perception of what mothers are "supposed to be". This can be a traumatizing experience for child, depending upon their age when the transition occurs, their inherited disposition, and personality. Some children are more resilient to change than others.

Mothers also may experience stress when their role changes. They may feel guilty or resentful if the change was not totally their choice. The change may have been necessary for economic reasons such as separation, divorce, a partner's illness, or loss of the primary breadwinner's job.

I recalled one of my neighbor's dilemmas. Frieda lived down the street from me and appeared to be part of a happily married couple with 2 young daughters, age 5 and 8. Jerome, the husband worked long hours and was seldom home. He was an executive with a large local company. His income was large. Jerome had always insisted that his wife, Frieda, stay at home with the children.

Frieda enjoyed being a stay-at-home parent and spent her time doing various activities with her children. She even became a Girl Scout leader.

One day, totally unexpectedly, Jerome came home from work and told Frieda that he needed to have a serious talk with her. He told her he had been seeing "someone else", had fallen in love with the other woman, and wanted to divorce Frieda. (Jerome moved out the next day and left Frieda and the girls.) Their divorce was final several months later.

Even though Frieda obtained a good settlement and child support, it was still necessary for her to get a job in order to support herself and the children within the same standard of living. She had been a teacher many years earlier and needed to take several college courses to update her license to teach. She was emotionally devastated by the whole experience.

I was one of Frieda's friends and observed firsthand how difficult it was for the girls to adjust to her absence and lowered level of involvement in their lives. Frieda told others how guilty and angry she felt about the change of her mothering role.

Social change is escalating. Awareness of the issues that impact how we raise children in the world today is critical to our understanding of what is needed as we mother our own children. Taking ourselves off the hot seat as well as taking our own mothers off the hot seat frees us to be more available to our children and others in our world. As we let go of any guilt related to parenting and anger toward our own mothers or fathers, we become free to find out who we really are as we individuate and take sole responsibility for what we do. Gerald Jampolsky, in his book "Forgiveness" stated "Forgiveness is the eraser that makes the hurtful past disappear".

Some "mothers" have changed their roles to expand their love and compassion beyond their family.

# Chapter 8

# THE EXPANSION
# OF MOTHERHOOD

*Mother's love*
*Always there's a circle*
*With my love just for you*
*And then there appears a circle for two*
*Sisters and brothers*
*And neighbors and friends*
*Experience the circle*
*That grows and expands*
*To envelop the earth*
*With a love that's so pure*
*It can pierce the darkness*
*And light up the world*

This book started with a fairy tale, with mothers on the hot seat. It is ending with good enough mothers off the hot seat in the new, ever changing reality of today.

Mothers are asked to cope with the many demands of today as they raise their children. There are demands upon their time, skills, intelligence, resilience, and courage. The demands are enormous and stressful. Mothers are a courageous hardworking, dedicated group of people who must be congratulated for their efforts to humanize not only their own children, but others beyond their families.

Motherhood is expanding. Years ago Harry Harlow began to study the basic needs that monkeys had right after birth if they were to develop normally. His experiments were not only interesting but somewhat startling.

## The Importance of Attention and Touch

This important study involved baby monkeys. Harlow actually probed the nature of love. He studied monkey love and repeatedly compared his subjects, the baby monkeys, to children.

Harlow took baby Rhesus monkeys away from their mothers at birth. Some to the babies were given a surrogate mother made of wire, others one of soft material over the wire. They were fed from a bottle which was attached to the surrogates. Monkeys who got their milk from a wire mother would leave the wire mother after feeding and go to a padded mother to spend their time.

As they got older, the monkeys who were fed by the wire mothers became totally antisocial and were not able to ever socialize normally with other monkeys. They were "mentally ill". When disruption in the form of a loud noise was generated, the monkeys who were fed by the cloth mothers ran to their cloth mother, clung to her and seemed to feel protected and safe. The monkeys who were fed by the wire mother did not retreat to the wire mother when scared. Instead, they threw themselves on the floor, clutched themselves, rocked back and forth, and screamed in terror. Their behavior closely resembled the behaviors of autistic and deprived children who are often observed in institutions, and similar as well to the pathological behavior of adults confined to mental hospitals. The monkeys fed by cloth mothers fared better. They were able to learn social skills if they were exposed to other normal monkeys later. This study helped us understand the importance of touch and softness while feeding in order to develop the feelings of safety they needed in order to develop. This is true for both animals and humans. His experiments helped us understand motherhood among animals at a beginning, basic level.

Rene Spitz, a psychiatrist, performed a research study of babies who were orphaned and living in a nursery. The babies were kept in cribs all day long. They received adequate food and were kept clean. (Their bottles were propped in order to feed them with minimal effort.) The babies did not receive cuddling, or have the experience of playing with their caregivers. The caretakers did not have time to do anything but provide minimum physical care for survival.

Spitz discovered that the incidence of death was much higher for those infants than infants raised by their own mothers. A large percentage died before the age of one. Those that survived failed to develop normal social skills and were developmentally delayed. They were unable to "attach" to other human beings in normal ways. His research helped psychologists understand the importance of a child attaching to his or her caregiver.

I watched videotapes of some of these children who appeared to be lying in their cribs, just staring. It brought tears to my eyes. One little girl in particular caught my eye. Her eyes were vacant as she seemed to be focused on her hand for about 15 minutes without moving. It was like she had "given up".

## The Importance of Parent-Child Bonding

Subsequent studies by John Bowlby taught us the importance of parent-child bonding. Bowlby taught us that the bond between mother and child is one of the most important connections they will have in life. It is permanent and critical for a baby's development. This bond is the basis of security in every individual. It is in some ways an irrational bond filled with emotion, deep and unchangeable. Bowlby stated that "a young child's hunger for his mother's love and presence is as great as his hunger for food." He described this bonding as attachment. Good enough mothers have healthy attachments with their children. Lack of attachment is harmful to the developing child. Children who are not "attached" to their mothers have difficulty throughout life establishing close relationships with others.

## Mothering Around the World

I had the opportunity to study different cultures over the years and have observed children with their mothers in many countries. Mother-child attachment is the same throughout the world.

In 1990 I was in India, meeting with spiritual leaders. During that trip, I had the opportunity to live with women in the Ashram of Sai Baba. Some of the women there had young children with them including infants. I lived for 4 days and nights with about 60 other women in a large dormitory where we all slept on mats on the floor with mosquito netting over each individual. Everyone there was waiting to meet with Sai Baba. I was the only Anglo-American woman present. I watched as the women with babies nursed them, cuddled them, and loved them. Several women were there with toddlers who were lovingly tended. I remember enjoying watching their tenderness. I thought to myself, "All people are the same".

On another trip, I was in New Zealand presenting a workshop. After the workshop, my hosts asked what I would like to see while I was in New Zealand. I mentioned the Maori natives of New Zealand were of interest to me. I was thrilled when I was later invited to become a member of a Maori tribe.

The formal ceremonies included first being serenaded by the tribe in their language. Next there were some speeches in the Maori language I could not understand, after which they requested in English that I give a speech to their group about who I was and what I did. After this, the Tribe sang to me in their language and then asked me to sing to them. I felt rather overwhelmed at this point and couldn't think about what to sing. As they waited I felt pressured, so sang "I've been working on the railroad". They all burst out laughing! That was when I realized that most or all of them could speak English. The last and most important part of the ceremony was profound. The whole tribe, consisting of about 100 people made a long, straight line. Their leader instructed me and demonstrated what I must do. I was shown how to become bonded with all of them. First, I must stand opposite the first person in the line, look deeply into their eyes, Touch foreheads, touch noses, and then simultaneously kiss each other on each cheek. After this, I was to work my way down the line, doing the same process with all 100 people. It took almost an hour and they all stood there politely until I was finished. Then, they applauded, and the tribal leader told me I was now one of them and had become a Maori. I somehow felt like I had too. I had bonded with all of them and to this day still feel part of them. Our connection ceremony involved touch, sharing, commitment, acceptance, and affection.

I was invited to spend an entire day in their compound as "one of them". During that day I observed some of my new "brothers and sisters" with their children. The children I saw were mostly with their mothers. I noted the same loving attention I had seen in India. I again thought mother love is the same everywhere.

When I spent time in West Africa studying traditional healing practices, I visited Nigeria and Sierra Leone. Babies there were usually wrapped up close to their mothers for constant body contact. I could see the love in the mother's eyes and observed their tender touches to their children.

This pattern of love repeated itself over and over as I traveled the world over a period of years. Some of the countries where I observed this were Russia, Canada, Cyprus, Israel, Brazil, Peru, Venezuela, Mexico, Tahiti, Australia, China, Thailand, France, Holland, England, Cyprus, Belgium, Sweden, Scotland, and Norway.

I determined that mother love is "Universal". Watching the distressed mothers who are victims of violence in Islamic countries reinforced that reality. These experiences helped me look at the beginning unit of focus, between mother and child.

It became clear that "motherhood" is found everywhere. Both men and women can exemplify it. Animals experience it also. It is based on unconditional love. Physical contact is an important part of it.

"Mothers" are responsible for humanizing the world. Human beings must be loved and feel loved in order to love others. They must learn to empathize with others and care what happens to them. They must be taught to look beyond their own needs to the needs of not only those around them, but beyond that, to the needs of the world.

## Degrees of Expansion

There are many different kinds of mothers and different degrees of focus for mothering. Some good enough mothers have the opportunity and/or desire to mother and share their unconditional love with only their own children. Others feel called to reach out to other adults and children beyond their own. Some mothers have the opportunity as well as desire to reach out beyond their locality and "mother" many others around the world. Some of these "mothers" may never have had their own children, but have "mothered" many others. It is important to have unconditional, compassionate love and support at all levels of focus.

On a trip to India I had the opportunity to work with Mother Theresa in Calcutta. Mother Theresa worked to help the dying. Another special project she had was to accept and care for abandoned children. She was a "mother" to the world. When I arrived at the entrance to her hospice, I was startled by, and felt a sense of horror when I saw 3 dead bodies wrapped in white sheets lying on the ground by her door. They had been placed there to await removal to the cremation fires. Their ashes would be scattered in the Ganges River.

I was there to volunteer a week of my time to help in any way I could. After an orientation by Mother Theresa, I had the opportunity to help her as she ministered to the dying. My nursing background helped me pull myself together and focus on doing whatever was needed. I fed and washed dying patients. Sometimes I just held their hands. It didn't seem to matter that I could not speak their language.

Mother Theresa was a humble woman. She not only directed all the volunteers, but worked herself as well. On more than one occasion, I saw her scrubbing the floor on her hands and knees. She never asked the volunteers to do that.

Mother Theresa also provided for children no one wanted. Many had been left on her doorstep by mothers in Calcutta who were starving and could not provide for their babies. There were rows and rows of cribs with children from infancy to about one year old. Volunteers like me, fed them, held and changed them. There were not enough volunteers to give them all the love they needed and no one wanted to adopt them. When I was there, I sometimes felt tearful and pained at the misery I witnessed. I felt helpless to fill all the needs I saw there but I felt awed by Mother Theresa. I could feel the love she bestowed upon all, including the volunteers.

I thought of two other people who personify the qualities of motherliness in the world, even though they never had children. The first is Oprah Winfrey. I have never met her, but have always been impressed by her generosity and loving demeanor. I believe she is a true humanitarian.

I discovered that she has a private charity, The Oprah Winfrey Foundation, through which she has awarded hundreds of grants to organizations that support the education and empowerment of women, children and families in the United States and around the world. She has donated millions of dollars toward providing a better education for students who have merit, but no means. She also visited orphanages and rural schools in South Africa and donated money for food, clothing, school supplies, books and toys as well as providing libraries and teacher education for 63 schools.

During a December 2000 visit with Nelson Mandela, Oprah pledged to build a school in South Africa. As that commitment broadened, she established the Oprah Winfrey Leadership Academy Foundation, to which she has contributed more than $40 million dollars toward the creation leadership Academy for Girls in South Africa. In 2012, Seventy Two students became the first graduating class of the school. I was also impressed when I learned that Oprah initiated the National child Protection Act in 1991. It established a national database of convicted child abusers. The above information does not include all her philanthropy. To my knowledge, she never had a child of her own.

As I mentioned earlier, men can also be Mothers to the world. When I thought about who it could be, I knew immediately. It was someone I knew.

In 1992 I traveled with a small group of people to India to explore spiritual leaders there. It was an intense and grueling trip. I had a profound experience one day that for some reason, makes me feel emotionsl as I recount it.

Our group of 8 people was traveling in a small, rickety van one day. We had decided to go to Dharmsala, a town in northern India on the side of a mountain where the Dalai Lama resides. We did not even know if he was in his ashram. It was decided that we would park the van in the town, spend several hours on our own, looking through the shops and talking with the natives if we chose and then meet at 5:00 p.m. in front of the Ashram. We agreed that if we got separated for any reason, we would meet at the Van.

I walked around the town alone for about 30 minutes and found that I was not interested in the shops and hadn't found any people to speak with. I decided to hike up the mountain to the Ashram just to make sure where it was. It took about 15 minutes. When I got to the gate, I heard the deep guttural chanting of Tibetan Monks.

I became transfixed as I listened. I had heard recordings of it in the past, but had never actually experienced it. I felt a tingling in my back and my chest expanded. I felt emotional as I was almost hypnotically drawn to opening the gate and entering. I walked down a path on the side of the mountain and came to another gate. A monk was there in saffron robes. I smiled at him and he smiled at me, wordlessly opening the gate. I continued to hear the chanting as I went down another path that led to a courtyard. There were people of all sorts in the courtyard who were prostrating themselves on the ground, getting up and repeating the process over and over. Some of them were dressed in peasant garb, others as young monks.

I watched for several moments, not sure what to do. Then I noticed another gate leading to another inner court yard which was in the direction of the guttural chanting. I went to that gate where another monk was standing. I smiled at him and he smiled at me, nodded and motioned me in. I felt like I was on a great adventure and being guided for some reason to continue, I had no expectations about where I was going, but felt safe somehow. Unbelievably, this courtyard had more people prostrating themselves over and over. The people there were wearing monk's robes of different kinds. I still didn't know what to do and felt like I was in some sort of alternate reality. I noticed yet another gate, entering I knew not what, except that I wanted to go there as that was the direction of the chanting. I went to the gate and received the same silent invitation to enter. This time it was different. I saw benches lining a room. The room was open to the sky. At one side were prayer wheels next to a side entrance to I knew not where. There were saffron robed monks sitting on the benches chanting. The gatekeeper motioned me to a seat between two chanting monks. I remember sitting down with a feeling of shock and gratitude. I somehow knew this was where I was supposed to be.

As I looked around I realized I was the only person there who was not a monk. More monks were arriving from the side entrance. As each came in, He spun the prayer wheel, sending a prayer to the universe, then sat down, and began chanting. The chanting got louder and louder. No one seemed to be astonished by my presence, but me.

The present time seemed timeless. Suddenly, another monk arrived and stood in front of the group. The chanting stopped. I recognized the Dalai Lama from pictures I had seen of him. He spoke for about 20 minutes. I couldn't understand a word, but that didn't matter a bit. Somehow I knew I belonged there, but had no clue why.

After the Dalai Lama spoke, He smiled at everyone and passed out candy to all of us. It felt like getting communion in some way. After this, he signaled that he was leaving. The monks began to line up on both sides of the walkway that they had all used when they entered. One monk motioned me to join them. I did so, wondering what would happen next. After we all lined up, the Dalai Lama came to the walkway and just stood for several minutes looking at the lines. I was somewhere in the middle. Suddenly, he walked over to me and never said a word, only looked deeply into my eyes for what seemed like an hour. I felt as if he had seen deeply into my soul and knew who I really was. I also felt connected to him and felt his love and purity; I was overwhelmed. After that connection was made, he smiled and nodded. He seemed to be satisfied with our interaction and he began to leave. The monks followed, I of course followed. There was a door and another gatekeeper. This time the gatekeeper stopped me and looked sad as he saw the tears running down my face.

I made my way down the mountain alone. It was dusk. The whole experience seemed surreal, and uplifting at the same time. By the time I got to the van, everyone else was there. No one had been able to get past the first courtyard but me.

This experience had a huge impact upon me. That night we got back to our hotel. I lay in my bed pondering the meaning of it all. I kept hearing guttural chanting in my sleep. I knew and still know that the Dalai Lama is a wonderful human being. Of all the spiritual leaders I have met, he was the only one I experienced as so pure of heart. He is filled with loving compassion and qualifies to me as a mother of the world.

The three "mothers of the world" I thought of, seemed like very different people on the surface. However, when I looked deeper, I realized they were much the same. All three have loving compassion for others, which goes beyond self, to envelope the world. All three have been willing to give of themselves and their resources to "pierce the darkness" and make a difference. Men and women who exemplify the mothering qualities at all the different degrees of expansion support the development of future adults who will be able to intervene in various ways to help solve our problems.

The world today needs individuals who are able to think differently from the previous generations. This is critically important as the escalating changes we are experiencing in society, demand innovative responses. The technological revolution has created a major "generation gap" in knowledge and adaptability never seen before. Our children must enter the future with problem solving and coping skills we may not fully understand.

The world has evolved into a community. If something affects people on one side of the world, it affects those on the other side. We are now all affected by Global Warming, fears of Asteroids destroying our world, other natural disasters such as earthquakes and volcanic eruptions, possibilities of nuclear war, pestilence, plagues, and Political unrest.

Since the technological revolution has enabled us to connect with others around the world, we can know their problems empathize with them. Some humanists may experience firsthand the pain of those affected by local turmoil far away. I identify myself as one of them and experience feelings of great sadness and helplessness as I watch the suffering in places like Liberia, Nigeria and Iran. Religious wars continue to develop around conflicting beliefs. Others are related to power and financial gain. Many people are concerned that we have so many people living on this planet; the earth will not be able to sustain the human race much longer. I wonder.

There are many reactions to these developments. I have communicated with men and women who are part of a growing movement to help people become aware of the "oneness" of all people around the world. These groups are based on a sense of universal love and peace. The mothers of the world are part of this thinking.

Mothers at every level are the "Teachers" of the world. They have the awesome responsibility to protect children's vulnerable psyches from negativity, violence, irresponsibility, and lack of empathy. Mothers are the ones who teach love, peace, responsibility, tolerance, and empathy. Their teachings can enable children everywhere to grow into human beings who can perceive our connectedness with all others and create a positive difference in our world of today and tomorrow. Mothers teach future generations to be human.

# Chapter 9

# PUTTING IT TOGETHER

A s I thought about my journey to discover who began to "bash" mothers and why, I realized I had learned many things in my conquest. I had considered the responsibility of society for causing some of the blame as well as other forces that could cause problems for children that mothers may be blamed for; such as child abuse, being a single mother, distorted memories, individual differences beginning in infancy, the technological revolution, and the stresses of social change.

It is evident that all of these forces may cause many problems for which mothers may be unfairly blamed. Understanding the above factors may not only facilitate understanding between parents and children, but help us define what good enough mothers can do at the different levels of expansion. Mothers may have an increased awareness of what type of intervention can help their specific relationship issues with their children, while mothers who choose to expand their mothering to others are needed to intervene at city, state, national levels and beyond. Mothers Against Drunk Drivers is an example of an intervention at a National Level.

## Effects of Blame

I had asked myself why my daughter was so upset with me for such a trivial incident. Part of the answer was normal separation and individuation. The other part was my going back to school when she needed me to be there. I learned that I had been feeling subconscious guilt for years about this. My subconscious guilt had not been good for either my daughter or me. I also realized that even though I decided a long time ago that I was not "perfect", part of me still wanted to be so. Bringing all these things into conscious awareness enabled me to work at "letting them go". I wondered how many of you have had similar or more intense problems with your mothers or children. This is an example of mothering issues that were related to my own specific problem.

I believe that some of you who have been reading this book may have been going through a similar process to mine. If you have children you may be wondering if you are or were a good enough mother. Some of you may decide you were or were not, and wonder why. If you never had children or are thinking of having one, you may be assessing whether or not you are capable of being a good enough mother. Another possibility is that you are deciding if your mother was a good enough mother. Some of you may decide your mother was not good enough. Some people who have experienced child abuse and neglect are afraid to have children as they may believe they do not know how to parent as they never experienced good parenting. It is possible to be a good enough mother even if you do not yet know how. You can learn. You may choose to attend some good parenting classes and also obtain therapy to help you determine when you are ready and what issues you must work through. Some women decide they cannot or do not choose to deal with the stresses of becoming a biological parent, but "mother" others nevertheless. Other women may decide they do not choose to mother anyone and desire to pursue other goals. Some readers may decide they deserve to be blamed as they abused, failed to protect, or failed to nurture their child.

It is possible that you may be angry at your adult children for either not meeting your expectations or for blaming you for their problems. You may feel like placing your child on that hot seat! All combinations are possible.

This book has defined the causes of mother blame and explored the effects of it. One reason that mothers usually receive more blame for children's problems than fathers is because they are traditionally the parent who is closer to the children and spends more time with them. Additionally, a mother can also serve as a scapegoat for social or physical ills that have not been explained or wish to be avoided. Scapegoating often seeks the most vulnerable target to blame. We, as a society must examine poverty, racism, the difficulties of finding meaningful work at a livable wage, the effects of technology on children, the lack of access to day care, and all the additional social problems that are present in our world today without using mothers as our scapegoats.

## Interventions

It is critical to understand the causes of mother bashing relevant to each individual case before applying appropriate interventions to remediate them. Interventions such as individual counseling, relationship counseling between parent and child, family counseling, or reading some of the excellent self-help books together with your mother or adult child are all helpful. (Some of which are listed in the Bibliography.) Awareness of the causes is the first step toward healing. The second step is to forgive yourself if you believe you made some mistakes or feel guilty as I did. Therapists knowledgeable about all the possible factors involved could help tailor interventions particularly relevant to you.

## Forgiveness

One of the most significant outcomes of my quest was to realize that the first goal to accomplish is to stop blaming yourself, even if you feel that you deserve blame. Continuing to blame yourself prevents change as well as inhibits your growth. In order to stop blaming yourself, you must first forgive yourself. This does not mean that you condone whatever you did. It only means you forgive yourself for it and can now move on to be the person you want to become.

I have been working on my own forgiveness for years. I continue to work on it as new things come up with either myself or others. Some of the things my mother did upset me. If I had not forgiven her long ago, I would have blocked myself from my own personal growth. During the writing of this book, I believe I have totally forgiven my daughter as well as myself for the pain we caused each other.

I was not always so forgiving in the past, especially when I thought I was "Perfect". I had a big break-through when I realized that forgiveness does not mean agreeing with the act or condoning an outrageous behavior. It does not mean you must be friends with the person or persons involved. You may decide to never see them again.

Forgiveness resolves the inner battles with our selves. It helps us to stop experiencing inner anger and blame. When we have forgiveness in our hearts, we can experience our true essence as love. It allows us to know who we really are.

When we forgive, much may be healed and we are able to feel connected to others and all life. We are open to experience the world without inner conflicts.

As a psychologist for more than 30 years, I have seen a number of people with various physical and emotional problems that were resolved by forgiveness. The following was one of those cases.

Abby was referred to me by both her medical doctor and psychiatrist. She had been married for the first time at the age of 35. She and her husband Ed were deeply in love. They were a wealthy couple and neither had to work. They took many trips around the world, had no children, and focused only on each other. Ed had been divorced for several years before they married. Both of them felt it was a "marriage made in heaven".

A year before I saw Abby, her husband Ed dropped dead of a heart attack at the tennis court during a tennis game. Abby was devastated and grief stricken. Her grief did not abate. After several months all her friends began to worry. Abby had lost an extreme amount of weight and looked anorexic. She vomited several times a day, usually after eating.

At her friend's insistence, she went to her medical doctor. He could find nothing physically wrong with her and referred her to a psychiatrist. Her psychiatrist diagnosed her as suffering from a pathological grief reaction and prescribed tranquilizers, antidepressants, and vitamins. He worked with her for several sessions to help her handle her grief. Abby continued to lose weight and vomit after every meal. No one had been able to help. The next step would be to put her in the hospital and feed her intravenously. If she was not improved in one week, that was the plan. This was when I received the referral.

When I realized the urgency of the situation, I set aside 3 hours for her on the first day, and two hours each day thereafter for the week I had to work with her. Abby weighed 78 lb. and was 5ft, 6 in tall. Since I realized there wasn't much time to do work, I decided to follow my intuition and said a little prayer to myself asking for guidance.

I wondered if Abby could be angry at anyone. I well knew that repressed anger can cause many physical symptoms as well as depression. On Abbey's first visit, I probed very directly, spending several hours trying to understand her life.

I found out something others had missed. Ed had always planned to change his will after his divorce, but had kept putting it off. When he died, his multi-million dollar estate went to his ex-wife whom he disliked. He had believed he was in perfect health and didn't need to "hurry". He was 39 years old and thought he would live "forever".

When I asked Abby if what he had done made her angry, she said "no, I knew he loved me." She started to cry. I knew I had to push hard because her life was at stake. I told her clearly that this had nothing to do with love. I explained that she could love him and be angry too. Abby looked startled and stopped crying. I sensed that I was on the right track and pursued further.

I asked Abby to take part in a Gestalt technique where she was instructed to visualize Ed sitting in the chair I placed across from her. Her task was to tell Ed that she was angry about his not changing the will, even though she loved him. Abby agreed to do this. She was scared and desperate.

She began slowly, and needed encouragement from me. Finally after about 10 minutes she began to vent absolute rage about what had occurred. This went on for about 45 minutes. She screamed, yelled expletives, and pounded a pillow. After she expressed her anger, she told Ed how much she loved him and then sobbed and sobbed for about 15 minutes. Abby then was able to compose herself. Her color looked better and she said she felt "relieved". I felt relieved too. The first session took 3 hours. I had an appointment with her for the following day.

The next morning Abby came in with a weak smile. She had been able to eat a light supper and had not vomited since our last session.

I saw Abby 2 hours a day for two days and then 1 hour a day for the last two days of the week. She had not vomited all week and gained 2 pounds. Her psychiatrist and I were both happy and hopeful. I continued to see her once a week after that for the next 4 months. She never vomited again and rapidly gained back her lost weight.

Abby's anger had been subconscious. Once she became aware of it and expressed it, her symptoms of vomiting were relieved. I helped her feel and express her anger until she got tired of it and felt ready to let it go.

Abby was still grieving to the degree that it inhibited her life. She did not want to go anywhere; felt depressed, cried all the time, and only wore black clothing. It had been about a year and a half since Ed had died. I hypothesized that even though she had released her anger, she had not forgiven Ed. Abby admitted that this was true and eventually decided that she was ready to work on forgiving Ed. Forgiveness happened quickly for her as it sometimes does when one is ready.

After forgiving Ed, Abby soon felt ready to resume a more normal life and complete her grieving in a healthier way. She called me 2 years later to tell me she was beginning a "new relationship". Forgiveness was the key for her to go on with her life.

I have found through long clinical experience with trauma victims that anger often overlays the pain they experienced in the past. True forgiveness cannot occur until that person can feel and express their anger in an appropriate way that hurts no one. Some ways to do this are pounding a pillow, writing a letter you do not send or, visualizing the perpetrator and telling them how you feel, even though they are not there. Children who have been truly abused usually severely repress their anger and rage. They may subconsciously be fearful that they may hurt someone with it. They cannot really forgive until they deal with their anger. Abby was not abused as a child and her anger was more easily accessible. She had been afraid she could not love Ed if she was angry about the money. It is important that anger not be repressed, before forgiving.

My personal experience with forgiveness has been that after I forgive someone, I feel much better and sometimes exuberant. However, later something may remind me of my anger at that person and I may feel unforgiving again. When that happens, I do it all over again and let it go. This may happen several times if it was a very painful and significant issue with someone I really cared about. My first husband and I divorced after 21 years of marriage and 3 children. At that time, I experienced a lot of anger and pain and often had nightmares about him. I tried not to think of him and repeatedly repressed my anger. However, it would emerge at night with my nightmares. We had both happily remarried and I moved to a different city. One night, 4 years after the divorce, I had another terrible nightmare about him. When I awoke, I consciously realized how angry I had been and made a decision in the middle of the night that I must forgive him in order to stop the nightmares. It all happened in an instant.

Over the years our relationship became friendlier and has evolved into a friendship. I am always happy to see him at family functions.

Sometimes, in order to gain perspective, it is helpful to think of how "not to do something". The following paragraph may help you do that.

These are directions on how to be unforgiving:

> Enjoy self-pity and faultfinding. Choose to be "right" rather than happy. Don't let go of being a victim. Believe you do not need or want peace of mind. Hold on to grievances and unforgiving thoughts and believe it makes the other person suffer. Refuse to believe that your emotional pain is caused only by your thoughts. Know without doubt that you do not have the power to choose the thoughts you put in your mind. Believe that holding on to anger will bring you what you want. Make decisions based on fear. Punish yourself because you know it has value. Know you do not deserve to be happy. See people as attacking you. Be suspicious and never see the light in anyone. Never let yourself see the light within yourself! Only count your hurts, not your blessings. Never give up your judgments. Take everything personally. Believe that anger is the most powerful force in the world. Always remember it is important to hurt yourself and others for the purpose of changing the other person. Never forgive!

If you follow the above directions for a lifetime, you will be miserable for a lifetime.

You must first forgive yourself, before you can forgive others. Almost everyone has something they are blaming themselves for. Forgiving yourself is a way to put a stop to self-blame. If you are willing, the best thing you can do for yourself is to forgive yourself and then begin the process of forgiving others, no matter what the wound. This will free you to make any changes you decide upon and to get help if necessary. Forgiveness frees us from the painful past.

I recommend Gerald Jampolsky's book, "Forgiveness, the Greatest Healer of All" (1999), to my patients who wish or need to forgive. He discusses two stages of forgiveness, the Preparation Phase and the Action Phase.

I will paraphrase his main points that may help you in this process. These are stepping stones to forgiveness. They are:

## The Preparation Stage: Changing your Beliefs

Meditation or prayer before starting is helpful. It simply means having a peaceful mind. To have a peaceful mind, you might find an image like a mountain lake to think about as you think about these principles. Do your best to look at the consequences of your choice to forgive or not to forgive, letting your heart help you decide.

1) Be open to the possibility of changing your beliefs about forgiveness.
2) Be willing to consider that you are a soul living temporarily in a body.
3) Find no value in self-pity
4) Find no value in being a faultfinder.
5) Choose to be happy, rather than "right".
6) Be willing to let go of being a victim.
7) Make peace of mind your only goal.

8) Look at everyone you meet as a teacher of forgiveness.
9) Believe that holding on to grievances and unforgiving thoughts is a way for you to suffer.
10) Recognize that any emotional pain you feel at this moment is caused only by your own thoughts.
11) Believe that you have the power to choose the thoughts you put in your mind.
12) Believe that holding on to anger does not bring you what you really want.
13) Believe that it is to your benefit to make decisions based on love, rather than fear.
14) Believe that there is no value in punishing yourself.
15) Believe you deserve to be happy.
16) Rather than seeing people as attacking you, see them as fearful and giving you a call of help for love.
17) Be willing to see the light of an innocent child in everyone you meet, regardless of the terrible things that they have done.
18) Be willing to see the light of the innocent child within you.
19) Be willing to count your blessings rather than your hurts.
20) Be willing to give up all your judgments.
21) Believe that love is the most powerful healing force in the world.
22) Believe that everyone you meet is a teacher of patience.
23) Believe that forgiveness is the key to happiness.

24) Believe that you can momentarily forget everything except the love that others have given you.

25) Treat every meeting you have, with every person you meet is a sacred relationship in which there is an opportunity to learn.

26) Let go of seeing any value in hurting or punishing the other person or yourself.

The next phase of forgiving is:

## The Action Stage: Choosing to forgive

You must be willing to move ahead in the forgiveness process. Know that you are willing to turn all your grievances and anger over to the highest truth within yourself. It is this higher truth within that allows you to transform your anger into love.

1) Decide you are no longer going to suffer the effects of your unforgiving thoughts being returned to you.

2) You may write a letter to the person you wish to forgive, expressing all of your feelings, and then tear it up.

3) You may choose to write poetry, putting thoughts and feelings into intimate and well-expressed words.

4) Remind yourself your only goal is peace of mind, not changing or punishing the other person.

5) If appropriate, be willing to see this person who hurt you as one of your strongest teachers, giving

you the opportunity to really learn if you have forgiven them.

6) Remember that in the process of forgiving the other person, you are forgiving yourself.

7) Begin to practice blessing and/or praying for the other person as well as yourself.

8) Remember that in forgiving, you are not agreeing with the other person or condoning their hurtful behavior.

9) Enjoy the happiness and peace that comes from forgiving.

Forgiving may take just an instant, years, or anything in between. I get better at it as I get older. I agree with Gerald Jampolsky's statement that, "Peace will come to the world when each of us takes the responsibility of forgiving everyone, including ourselves completely". "Mothers" can help that happen.

## Responsibility

As we become who we really are, we must decide how we wish to conduct our lives. It is also our responsibility to not only choose to forgive, but how to live. This may seem overwhelming in these times. We must decide how to live. There are many choices to be made. The following are, I believe, among the most important:

The first is to be honest or dishonest with one's self and others.

The second is the choice of a life partner, partners, or no partner.

The third is the choice of your life's work.

The fourth choice is whether or not to allow yourself to experience loving compassion for others and, if you do, how far to expand it.

Carl Jung's statement, "It is really the individual's task to differentiate himself from all the others and stand on his own feet" is a reminder to all of us what our goal for ourselves must be. Only then can we truly have a clear, comfortable relationship with our mothers and our children as well as all the significant others in our lives and beyond. Mothers and children must be free to meet the ever growing and changing challenges of the future either separately or together. What can happen next is a beginning, not an ending!

Blaming is like a rope that ties you in knots and paralyzes your progress toward being the best you can be. Ending blame for yourself, your mother, your children, or anyone else who has hurt you (no matter how much they deserve it); invites you to pass through a gate to the wonderous, exciting path of growing self awareness. As you follow this path; you must confront all aspects of yourself, both the good and the bad. This is the path to finding out who you really are. It can enable you to fulfill your wildest dreams and be at peace with yourself and the world. The choice to proceed is yours alone.

We need more research to develop better understanding between mothers and adult children. The following pages have a questionnaire that may be taken on my web site. Please help us by filling it out. Results will be provided on my web site every month.

# Thank You!

# SURVEY ON MOTHER BLAME

You are invited to take the following survey to help us obtain much needed research about "Mothering". The survey will take about 5 minutes and can be completed easily on my website. ([www.drnancyperryauthor.com](www.drnancyperryauthor.com))

This survey may be taken by anyone over the age of 18. (You do not need to have read the book, 'Mother Bashing, does she deserve it?")

Have you read the book on Mother Bashing? Yes__ No__

Please check the following that pertain to you:

Male__ Female__ Age____ Reside in the U.S __
Reside elsewhere __
If residing elsewhere, where_____
Have lived in the US. in the past Yes__ No___

Non-Hispanic, White or Euro-American__
Black, Afro-Caribbean or Afro-American__
Latino or Hispanic American__
East Asian or Asian American__
South Asian or Indian American__
Middle Eastern or Arab American__
Native American or Alaskan Native__

You should complete both sections if you have a child 18 years of age or older. If you have no adult children, take only the section for children.

# SECTION FOR MOTHERS

Mothers may be defined as anyone who performed a mother role in raising their children. (This role could be performed by both men and women. It may include grandparents, biological mothers, biological fathers, partners, adoptive parents, step parents, Extended family, Neighbors, a married couple, or anyone else fulfilling this role).

1.) Have one or more of your adult children told you that you have done or said something to them before the age of 18 that they believe has caused major damage in their life? Yes___ No___

2.) If you said yes, rate the level of emotional pain you experienced as a result of this.

Mild or none               Moderate                    Severe

_1_____2_____3_____4_____5_

Please check one

3.) Have one or more of your adult children appeared to withdraw from you emotionally by such behaviors as "shutting you out, withdrawing, ignoring, emotional coldness, or avoiding you"? Yes__ No__

4.) If you answered yes, rate the level of emotional pain you experienced as a result of this.

Mild or none                Moderate                Severe

_1_____2_____3_____4_____5_

Please check one

5.) Do you believe your adult children really understand who you are as a person? Yes__ No__

6.) If you answered No, rate the level of emotional pain you experienced as a result of this.

Mild or none                Moderate                Severe

_1_____2_____3_____4_____5_

Please check one

# SECTION FOR CHILDREN

Do not take this section if you mother died before you were 18.

1) Do you believe your mother has done or said something or not done or said to you before the age of 18 that has caused major problems for you in your life? Yes__ No__
2) If you answered yes, please rate the level of emotional pain you experienced as a result of this.

Mild or none           Moderate            Severe

_1_____2_____3_____4_____5_

Please check one

3) Do you believe your mother appeared to withdraw from you emotionally when you were a child by such behaviors as "shutting you out, ignoring, emotional coldness, avoiding or actually abandoning you?" Yes__ No__
4) If you answered yes, please rate the level of emotional pain you experienced as a result of this.

Mild or none           Moderate            Severe

_1_____2_____3_____4_____5_

Please check one

5) Do you believe your mother really understands who you are as a person since you became an adult? Yes__ No__

6) If you answered No, please rate the level of emotional pain you experienced as a result of this.

Mild or none               Moderate             Severe

_1_____2_____3_____4_____5_

Please check one

7) Is your mother deceased? Yes__ No__

8) I you answered Yes, How old were you when she died? _____

If you read this book before taking this survey, do you believe it affected your responses? Yes__ No__

9) If you answered yes, explain how.

_____
_____
_____
_____

7) Tell us your story. Is there any other information you would like us to know? I will use this information in later books.

_____
_____
_____
_____

Thank you for completing the survey!

# Bibliography

Adams, Jane. 2003. *When Our Grown Kids Disappoint Us-Letting Go of Their Problems, Loving Them Anyway and Getting on with Our Lives New York: Free Press.*

Alcorn, Katrina. 2013. *Maxed Out, American Moms On the Brink* Berkley: Seal Press.

Bottke, Allison. 2008. *Setting Boundaries With Your Adult Children* Eugene, Oregon: Harvest House.

Bowlby, J. 1980. *Loss, Sadness and Depression.* Vol 3 of *Attachment and Loss* London: Hogarth p 185.

Caplan, Paula J. 2000. *Don't Blame Mother-Mending the Mother-Daughter Relationship* New York: Routledge.

Coleman, Joshua. 2008. *When Parents Hurt* New York: HarperCollins.

Colombo, John. and Fagen, Jeffrey., Eds. 1990. *Individual Differences in Infancy: Reliability, Stability, Prediction* Hillesdale, New Jersey: Lawrence Erlbaum Associates.

Ehlers, A., and Clark, E.M. 2000. "A Cognitive Modes of Posttraumatic Stress Disorder" *Behavior Research and Therapy.* 38, 319-45.

Ford, Martin. 2009. *The Lights in the Tunnel* United States: Acculant Publishing.

Freud, Sigmund. 1905. *The Sexual Enlightenment of Children.* New York: Macmillin Company

Gazzanign, M.S. 1998. "The Split Brain Revisited" *Scientific American* 270. 50-55.

Harlow, Harry F. "Love in Infant Monkeys."200 *Scientific American* (June, 1959): 68, 70, 72-73, 74.

Hoghughi, M. and Speight, N.P.1998 "Good Enough Parenting for all Children, a Strategy for a Healthier Society" *Archives of Disease in Childhood* London: 78: 293-296.

Isay, Jane. 2007. *Walking On Eggshells* New York: Random House.

Jampolsky, Gerald. *Forgiveness, the Greatest Healer of all*. Hillsboro, Oregon: Beyond Words publishing.

Jung, Carl. 1982. *Memories, Dreams, and Reflections* New York: Vintage Books.

Kunst, Jennifer. 2012. "A Headshrinkers Guide to the Galaxy" *Psychology Today* (May).

Mahler, M., Pine F. and Bergman, A. 1975. *The Psychological Birth of the Human Infant New York: Basic Books*.

McCoy, Monica and Keen, M. 2014 *Child Abuse and Neglect* New York: Psychology Press.

Merrill, Deborah M. 2011. *When Your Children Marry* Lanham, Maryland: Roman and Littlefield.

Morgan, E., Kuykendall, C. 1997. *What Every Child Needs* Colorado Springs: Alive Communications.

Neill, John M.C. 1990. "Whatever Became of the Schizophrenic Mother?" American *Journal of Psychotherapy:* Vol. XLIV No.4 p.499-505.

Richmond, Gary. *Successful Single Parenting* Eugene, Oregon: Harvest House.

Schacter, D. 2001. *The Seven Sins of Memory* New York: Houghton Mifflin.

Taylor S.E. and Brown, J.D. 1988. "Illusion and Well-Being: A Social and Psychological Perspective on Mental Health." *Psychological Bulletin:* 103, 193-210.

Toffler, Alvin. 1971. *Future Shock* New York: Bantum Books.

Utting, D, Bright, J. and Henricson, C. *Crime and the Family-Improving Childrearing and preventing delinquency* London: Family Policy Centre (June, 1993)

United States Census Bureau.2011. *Custodial Mothers and Fathers and Their Child Support* Washington, DC.

Uzendoorn, Marinus H. 1994. *Attachment in Context, Kibbutz Childrearing A Historical Experiment.* Paper presented at the International Society for The Study of Behavioral Development: Amsterdam.

Wegner, Daniel, M. 1944. "Iconic Processes of Mental control." *Psychological Review:* 101, 34-52.

Winnicott, D.W. 1952. *Letter to Roger Money-Kyrle, 27 November in the Spontaneous Gesture: Selected Letters of D.W. Winnicott* London: Karmic Books, 1987, pp 38-43.

Winnicott, D.W., 1988. *Babies and Their Mothers* London: Free Association Books.

Winnicott, D.W. 1965. *The Maturational Processes and the Facilitating Environment* London: Karmac books, 2005.

Wylie, Philip. 1955. *Generation of Vipers* New York: Rinehart.

# Author Bio

Dr. Nancy E. Perry is a Clinical Psychologist as well as a Registered Nurse and an Artist. She earned her Nursing, M.A. and Ph.D. degrees at the Ohio State University and an Associate' s Degree in Fine Arts at the Santa Fe Community College. Dr. Perry has served on the faculty of the Ohio State University, The University of Wisconsin, and the Wisconsin Professional School of Psychology.

Her clinical practice has included: Marriage and Family Therapy, Individual Therapy, and the treatment of Trauma Victims. She is a recognized authority in the treatment of Dissociative Disorders and has presented papers and workshops in many countries around the world. She is currently devoting most of her time to writing, painting and consultations. Dr. Perry resides in Santa Fe, New Mexico with her husband. She is the mother of three children.

CPSIA information can be obtained at www.ICGtesting.com
Printed in the USA
LVOW04*2242150115

423053LV00001B/1/P